A Multiple Intelligences Road To An ELT Classroom

by

Michael Berman
Education Project Manager,
Anglo-European Study Tours

Crown House Publishing Limited

First published in the UK by

Crown House Publishing Limited
Crown Buildings
Bancyfelin
Carmarthen
Wales

© Michael Berman 1998

The right of Michael Berman to be identified as the author of this work has been asserted by
him in accordance with the Copyright, Designs and Patents Act 1988.

First published 1998.

British Library of Cataloguing-in-Publication Data
A catalogue entry for this book is available
from the British Library.

ISBN 1899836233

Printed and bound in Wales by
WBC Book Manufacturers,
Waterton Industrial Estates,
Bridgend, Mid Glamorgan.

Table of Contents

Acknowledgements

The author thanks the following for permission to reproduce copyright material:

Zephyr Press, PO Box 66006, Tucson AZ 85728-6006 for permission to use extracts from *The Magical Classroom* by F. Noah Gordon

Network Educational Press, PO Box 635, Stafford ST16 1BF for permission to use extracts from *Accelerated Learning In The Classroom* by Alistair Smith

Connla And The Fairy Maiden and **Bedd Gelert** taken from *Celtic Fairy Tales* collected by Joseph Jacobs, 1968, Dover Publications Inc., 180 Varick Street, New York NY 10014

Love Is, copyright 1986, Adrian Henri. Reproduced by permission of the author, c/o Rogers, Coleridge & White Ltd., 20 Powis Mews, London W11 1JN

Yours, Mine, Ours - Whose Job Is It? (page 7) adapted by permission of SkyLight Training and Publishing Inc. (Arlington Heights, Illinois, USA) from *A Multiple Intelligences Road To A Quality Classroom* by Sally Berman, © 1998 by IRI/SkyLight Training and Publishing Inc.

Extracts from *Spinning Inward* by Maureen Murdoch, 1987, reprinted by arrangement with Shambhala Publications Inc., Boston

Why The Crab Has No Head taken from *Cordillera Tales* by Maria Luisa B. Aguilar-Carino, New Day Publishers, 11 Lands ST., Project 6, P.O. Box 167, 1100 Quezon City, Philippines

The Boy With The Magic Brush taken from *Chinese Folk Tales* by Howard Giskin - 1997, NTC Publishing Group, PO Box 73437, Chicago, Illinois, 60673 3437 USA

A Fable Of A Bird And Her Chicks taken from *The Second Virago Book Of Fairy Tales* - 1992, Virago Press Ltd

Adapted extracts from *Target Fluency* by Michael Hager - 1996, Metamorphous Press, P.O. Box 10616, Portland OR 97210

If any other copyright holders have been inadvertently overlooked, the author will be pleased to make the necessary arrangements at the first opportunity.

Introduction

The idea for the title was taken from *A Multiple Intelligences Road To A Quality Classroom* - a book by Sally Berman (no relation) published by IRI/Skylight Training and Publishing Inc., 1995. Sally Berman is a retired high school chemistry teacher. Although some of the materials from that book can be adapted for use in English Language Teaching and it is well worth reading, it was not written with ELT in mind.

Anyone who has read the work of Howard Gardner, the educational psychologist, cannot fail to recognise the relevance of Multiple Intelligences Theory to all forms of teaching, and this book is the first to apply it to English Language Teaching. MI Theory provides a much more comprehensive definition of intelligence than the traditional Binet model upon which IQ tests are based and recognises that intelligence is something that can be developed rather than something fixed.

The opening chapter provides an outline of this theory and is followed by chapters on how to cater for each of the eight intelligence types in the ELT classroom. The intention in each case is to illustrate how the theory can be applied in practice. The conclusion presents an alternative teaching model which incorporates MI Theory and other Accelerated Learning techniques such as Neuro-Linguistic Programming, Educational Kinesiology and Suggestopedia. There is also an appendix which deals with how to cater for young learners.

Our own strengths and weaknesses are, not surprisingly, reflected in our teaching styles. This is why it is so important for us as teachers to be aware of our individual intelligence profiles so we can make adaptations in class to ensure we reach everyone in the group. I hope as you read through this book my own weaknesses will not become too apparent to you!

Unit 1: Learning Styles And Intelligence Types

Neuro-Linguistic Programming (or NLP) is a set of guiding principles, attitudes and techniques that enable you to change or eliminate behaviour patterns. It describes the dynamic between the mind and language and how their interplay "programmes" our behaviour.

It began in the 1970s with John Grinder and Richard Bandler who explored how to model excellence by closely observing three highly successful therapists at work. The process they used was "modelling" - relying not only on what the three thought they were doing, but on the patterns of language and behaviour they actually used. The two researchers then tried out these same patterns themselves and developed strategies to pass them on to others.

One useful idea from NLP is that we take in information chiefly through the eye, ear and movement, and that we each have our own preferred learning style. As communicators we need to work to the varied strengths of our audience and as teachers we need to work to the varied strengths of our students, rather than get stuck in our own preferred style and impose this on others. The aim is not to put people into categories, which is to limit potential, but to teach multi-modally and reach everyone in the group.

"When we process information internally, we can do it visually, auditorily, kinesthetically, olfactorily or gustatorily. As you read the word 'circus', you may know what it means by seeing images of circus rings, elephants or trapeze artists; by hearing carnival music; by feeling excited; or by smelling and tasting popcorn or cotton candy. It is possible to access the meaning of a word in any one, or any combination, of the five sensory channels." (From *Trance Formations* by John Grinder & Richard Bandler, 1981.)

By identifying a person's preferred learning style and mirroring it, it then becomes possible to influence that person without his or her being aware of the process. In the hands of unscrupulous practitioners, the technique can be used to exploit people and is open to misuse. For this reason, it is not my intention to sell NLP to anyone. However, the awareness of learning styles clearly has important implications for us as teachers. Whether we follow the PPP model (presentation, controlled practice, production), the ARC model (authentic use, restricted use, clarification) developed by Jim Scrivener or the OHE model (observation, hypothesis, experiment) recommended by Michael Lewis is of secondary importance. Unless we cater for the learning styles of the students we teach, none of these models will succeed in reaching everyone in the group.

So how to identify learning styles and how to cater for them? Grinder and Bandler propose identifying learning styles from eye movements or "eye accessing cues". This may be appropriate in a one-to-one relationship with a client in therapy but impractical in the classroom.

An alternative approach is to pay attention to the kind of language the students use – verbal and non-verbal. For example, the sort of person who says "I see what you mean" is more than likely to be predominantly visual. The type of person who remarks "I hear what you're saying to me" is probably an auditory learner. The kind of person who uses expressions such as "what you said really grabs me" could well be a kinesthetic learner. Auditory learners also tend to talk over you and kinesthetic learners will be restless and constantly fidgeting.

Another way of identifying the learning styles of your students is by giving them a questionnaire to complete, and one designed for this purpose is presented below. Some suggestions as to how to cater for the learning styles are included in the analysis that follows the questions.

What Kind Of Learner Are You?

1. **How can other people best interpret your emotions?**
   a. through your facial expressions
   b. from the quality of your voice
   c. through your general body language

2. **How do you manage to keep up with current events?**
   a. by reading the newspaper thoroughly when you have the time
   b. by listening to the radio or watching the TV news
   c. by quickly reading the paper or spending just a few minutes watching the TV news

3. **What sort of driver (or passenger) are you?**
   a. you frequently check the rear view mirror and watch the road carefully
   b. you turn on the radio as soon as you get into the car
   c. you can't get comfortable in the seat and continually shift position

4. **How do you prefer to conduct business?**
   a. by having face-to-face meetings or writing letters
   b. over the phone because it saves time
   c. by talking while you are walking, jogging or doing something else physical

5. **How do you react when you're angry?**
   a. by clamming up and giving others the silent treatment
   b. by quickly letting others know when you're angry
   c. by clenching your fists, grasping something tightly or storming off

6. **How would you describe the way you dress?**
   a. a neat and tidy dresser
   b. a sensible dresser
   c. a comfortable dresser

7. **What do you think the best way is to discipline a child?**
   a. to isolate the child by separating him/her from the group
   b. to reason with the child and discuss the situation
   c. to use acceptable forms of corporal punishment

8. **How do you behave at meetings?**
   a. you come prepared with notes and displays
   b. you enjoy discussing issues and hearing other points of view
   c. you would rather be somewhere else and so spend your time doodling

9. **What do you like doing in your free time?**
   a. watching TV or going to the cinema
   b. listening to the radio, going to a concert or playing a musical instrument
   c. engaging in a physical activity of some kind

10. What do you consider to be the best way of rewarding students?
    a. writing positive comments on their work
    b. giving oral praise to the student
    c. a pat on the back, a hug, or some other appropriate physical action

What Your Score Means

If most of your answers are A, then your modality strength is visual. In other words, you learn through seeing things and you like everything to be written down on paper. In a classroom, having notes and the use of visual aids will help you.

If most of your answers are B, your modality strength is auditory. In other words, you learn through listening. In a classroom you will want to hear the new language, and listening to music could well be helpful.

If most of your answers are C, your modality strength is kinesthetic. In other words, you learn on the move or through movement. Sitting passively in a classroom is unlikely to appeal to you but you'll probably respond well to the use of games and role-play.

(taken from *? R U* by Michael Berman, 1995)

What is MENSA and who is eligible to become a member?

MENSA is an exclusive club for people with a high IQ or Intelligence Quotient. IQ tests were developed by Binet early this century and were frequently used to assess the potential of children in schools until quite recently. Tests of this type, however, have now fallen into disrepute. All they test is linguistic and logical-mathematical intelligence, and this traditional definition of intelligence is now regarded as too narrow. The educational psychologist largely responsible for this change of attitude is Howard Gardner, the creator of the *Multiple Intelligences Theory*.

Gardner has identified eight intelligence types so far and our intelligence profiles consist of combinations of the different types: linguistic, logical-mathematical, spatial, bodily-kinesthetic, musical, interpersonal – the way we relate to others, intrapersonal - our ability to self-evaluate, and naturalist – our talent for classifying and categorising.

What are the implications of this theory for teachers? It is clear that unless we teach multi-modally and cater for all the intelligence types in each of our lessons, we will fail to reach all the learners in the group, whichever approach to teaching we adopt. It is also apparent that if we impose learning styles on our students, they will prove to be ineffective. Learners with highly developed spatial intelligence, for example, will respond to the use of diagrams to record new vocabulary whereas this technique may have little or no impact on the rest of us.

Does the fact that we each have a unique profile mean that we should plan individual lessons for everyone in the class to take this into account? Clearly this would be impractical and so the solution lies in including material designed to appeal to each of the seven types in every lesson we give.

There follows a list of activities designed to develop the eight intelligences. You might like to try to categorise them under the eight different headings before you check the answers to see if you were correct.

- background music
- charts
- completing worksheets
- diagrams
- group discussions
- learner diaries
- mind maps
- personal goal setting
- reading articles & books
- self-study
- videos

- brain gym
- circle dancing
- craftwork
- giving presentations
- groupwork
- listening to lectures
- pairwork
- problem solving
- reflective learning activities
- songs
- visualisations

- brainstorming
- classifying & categorising activities
- guided discovery
- jazz chants
- logic puzzles
- peer teaching
- project work
- role-play
- storytelling
- word games

Activities To Develop The Eight Intelligences

Linguistic Intelligence:

- group discussions
- completing worksheets
- giving presentations
- listening to lectures

- reading
- wordbuilding games
- storytelling

Logical-mathematical Intelligence:

- logic puzzles
- logical-sequential presentations

- problem solving
- guided discovery

Spatial Intelligence:

- charts
- mind maps
- visualisations

- diagrams
- videos

Bodily-kinesthetic Intelligence:

- circle dancing
- brain gym

- relaxation exercises
- craftwork

Musical Intelligence:

- songs
- jazz chants

- background music

Interpersonal Intelligence:

- groupwork
- brainstorming

- pairwork
- peer teaching

Intrapersonal Intelligence:

- project work
- learner diaries
- reflective learning activities

- self-study
- personal goal setting

Naturalist Intelligence:

- classifying & categorising activities

- background music - in the form of sounds created in the natural world

The following **Multiple Intelligences Checklist** for EFL students is adapted from an article by Mary Ann Christison published in the *MEXTESOL* (Mexican branch of the *American Teachers Of English To Speakers Of Other Languages*) *Journal*. When the original article was published, only seven intelligence types had been identified. More recently, the naturalist intelligence has been added to the list and the checklist has been rewritten to take this into account.

Multiple Intelligences Checklist. Rank each statement 0, 1, or 2. Write 0 if you disagree with the statement and write 2 if you strongly agree. Write 1 if you are somewhere in between.

Linguistic Intelligence

___ 1. I like to read books, magazines and newspapers

___ 2. I consider myself a good reader

___ 3. I like to tell jokes and stories

___ 4. I can remember people's names easily

___ 5. I like to recite tongue twisters

___ 6. I have a good vocabulary in my native language

Logical-Mathematical Intelligence

___ 1. I often do calculations in my head

___ 2. I'm good at chess and/or draughts

___ 3. I like to put things into categories

___ 4. I like to play number games

___ 5. I love to play around with computers

___ 6. I ask lots of questions about how things work

Spatial Intelligence

___ 1. I can read maps easily

___ 2. I enjoy art activities

___ 3. I can draw well

___ 4. Videos and slides really help me to learn new information

___ 5. I love books with pictures

___ 6. I enjoy putting puzzles together

Bodily-Kinesthetic Intelligence

___ 1. It's hard for me to sit quietly for a long time

___ 2. It's easy for me to copy exactly what other people do

___ 3. I'm good at sewing, woodwork, building or mechanics

___ 4. I'm good at sports

___ 5. I enjoy working with my hands - working with clay or model-making, for example

___ 6. I enjoy physical exercise

Musical Intelligence

__ 1. I can hum the tunes to lots of songs

__ 2. I'm a good singer

__ 3. I play a musical instrument or sing in a choir

__ 4. I can tell when music sounds off-key

__ 5. I often tap rhythmically on the table or desk

__ 6. I often sing songs

Interpersonal Intelligence

__ 1. I'm often the leader in activities

__ 2. I enjoy talking to my friends

__ 3. I often help my friends

__ 4. My friends often talk to me about their problems

__ 5. I've got a lot of friends

__ 6. I'm a member of several clubs

Intrapersonal Intelligence

__ 1. I go to the cinema alone

__ 2. I go to the library alone to study

__ 3. I can tell you some things I'm good at doing

__ 4. I like to spend time alone

__ 5. My friends find some of my actions strange sometimes

__ 6. I learn from my mistakes

Naturalist Intelligence

__ 1. I spend a lot of time outdoors

__ 2. I enjoy listening to the sounds created in the natural world - birdsong, for example

__ 3. I can identify plantlife and animal species

__ 4. I can distinguish between poisonous and non-poisonous snakes and/or between poisonous and edible mushrooms

__ 5. I enjoy observing plants and/or collecting rocks

__ 6. I've got green fingers - I keep pot plants at home and have an interest in gardening, for example

There follows an activity designed to promote a greater sense of learner independence and which caters for four of the intelligence types. It is adapted from a lesson plan in *A Multiple Intelligences Road To A Quality Classroom* by Sally Berman (1995). The students use their spatial intelligence to complete the diagram, their interpersonal intelligence to work in groups, their linguistic intelligence to examine the list of responsibilities, and their naturalist intelligence to classify and categorise the statements.

Yours, Mine, Ours - Whose Job Is It?

Work in groups and decide where to place the following items in the Venn diagram. Compare your version with the versions of the other groups to reach a consensus, then fill in a copy of the diagram to display on the noticeboard.

1   Marking the register
2   Evaluating work
3   Maintaining order in the classroom
4   Treating others with respect
5   Being punctual
6   Explaining/teaching material
7   Being sure I learn
8   Tutoring

9   Helping others
10 Keeping a record of the material covered

11 Attending regularly
12 Being a course content expert
13 Developing the programme of study
14 Being prepared for class
15 Deciding on the course content
16 Preparing the course content
17 Getting what I want responsibly
18 Being sure I know what I miss when I'm absent

The Teacher's Role   **The Student's Role**

There has been a lot of attention paid recently to the importance of **emotional intelligence** as a result of Daniel Goleman's best-seller with that title (1996). Emotional intelligence is merely an expansion of Gardner's interpersonal and intrapersonal intelligences. Salovey & Mayer then subsume Gardner's personal intelligences in their basic definition of emotional intelligence, expanding these abilities into five main domains:

1. Knowing one's emotions (self-awareness)
2. Managing emotions
3. Motivating oneself
4. Recognizing emotions in others
5. Handling relationships

In conclusion, two basic forms of intelligence can be identified – rational and emotional – and our achievement is determined by both. As teachers we need to be aware of this because intellect cannot work at its best without emotional intelligence and *vice versa*. Creating a conducive classroom atmosphere in which students feel relaxed and can produce their best work, and catering for their preferred learning styles and intelligence types, are probably even more important than the teaching model we choose to adopt. However, these seem to be considerations that are neglected on most teacher training courses and it is high time we redressed the balance.

If you are interested in finding out more about the subject, the following books are recommended:

- *Frogs Into Princes* by John Grinder & Richard Bandler - Real People Press, 1979
- *Trance Formations* by John Grinder & Richard Bandler - Real People Press, 1981
- *In Your Hands* by Jane Revell & Susan Norman - Saffire Press, 1997
- *Frames of Mind* by Howard Gardner - Paladin, 1983
- *A Multiple Intelligences Road To A Quality Classroom* by Sally Berman - IRI/Skylight Training and Publishing Inc., 1995
- *Emotional Intelligence* by Daniel Goleman - Bloomsbury, 1996
- *Accelerated Learning In The Classroom* by Alistair Smith - Network Educational Press, 1996

Unit 2: How To Cater For Kinesthetic Intelligence

VAKOG is a mnemonic device used in Neuro-Linguistic Programming to refer to the main representational styles - visual, auditory, kinesthetic, olfactory and gustatory. **VAK** refers to the three primary learning styles – visual, auditory and kinesthetic. Unless you cater for these three styles in the classroom, you can never be sure of reaching all the students in the group. The kinesthetic students, for example, learn through movement. Unless they have an opportunity to do so at some point during the lesson, they are unlikely to get much out of the experience except for a sense of frustration. An average classroom of learners will include twenty-nine percent who are visual learners, thirty-four percent who are auditory, and thirty-seven percent who are kinesthetic. NLP has successfully demonstrated that communication between two people takes place in the dominant representational system so we need to have a variety of strategies or our communication is largely with only one group. The activities presented below are all designed to cater for those of our students who learn through movement. First of all, here are six ways of starting a lesson or providing a break halfway through:

1. "Everybody stand up please. I'd like you to organise yourselves according to the size of your shoes - the smallest foot on my left, the largest foot on my right ... . Now sit down and form a pair with the person next to you to work on the following activity."

2. "Everybody stand up please. I'm going to read out a list of adjectives and I'd like you to sit down when you hear an adjective that describes the way you're feeling." (If anyone is still standing when you come to the end of your list, then ask them to produce an adjective of their own.)

3. "Everybody stand up please. I'd like you to organise yourselves according to how many brothers and sisters you have - the smallest family on my left and the largest family on my right ... . Now sit down and form a pair with the person next to you to work on the following activity."

4. "Everybody stand up please. I'd like you to sit down when I come to the time you went to bed last night." (Start calling out the time in fifteen-minute intervals from 8 o'clock onwards until everyone is seated.)

5. "Everybody stand up please. I'd like you to find the person whose birthday is closest to yours ... . Now sit down and form a pair with that person to work on the following activity."

6. "Everybody stand up please. I'd like you to organise yourselves alphabetically according to your first names (or surnames) - A on my left and Z on my right ... . Now sit down and form a pair with the person next to you."

How many more suggestions can you come up with for getting students out of their chairs and for re-arranging the pairings or groupings in the class?

When working on pronunciation, kinesthetic reinforcement can be provided by having students trace intonational contours with their arms and fingers as they say a given utterance, or by identifying the number of syllables by holding up the corresponding number of fingers as they pronounce polysyllabic words or phrases. Another possibility is for the learners to clap their hands or snap their fingers to the rhythm of the passage while the teacher reads. They can then practise reading as their peers tap out the rhythm.

With students who have difficulty with stress patterns, you can have them stand in front of you and place both their palms facing outwards against yours. Ask them to put steady pressure against your hands, then say whatever you want them to say using pressure to help them feel the differing stress levels. Invite them to close their eyes during the process to facilitate internal focus. Tell them to begin to repeat what they hear as soon as they think they feel it. Repeat the process until you can hear what you want and until you can see from their faces that they feel they have it.

Another means of providing kinesthetic reinforcement is by making use of a carton of eggs. Pick one out (hardboiled, but the learners believe it to be raw!) and with a marker pen draw the phoneme you want to practise on the shell. Elicit the sound from the class; then throw the egg to one of the students who has to say a word containing the sound. This student then throws the egg to someone else, who must repeat the first word and add another of his/her own, and so on.

You can also use jazz chants, where students, working in pairs, clap or beat the rhythm of the utterance for each other as they repeat the chant. This activity brings together word stress, sentence stress, contractions, linking and intonation. Songs such as the "Hokey Cokey" can be useful for kinesthetic reinforcement too. The learners form a circle to sing or act it out with the teacher. This is particularly effective for linking sounds - "You put your left arm in, left arm out," etc.

The game of "Emotional Intonation" provides a useful activity to cater for the kinesthetic intelligence type. Elicit and board different emotional states – boredom, surprise, excitement and anger, for example. Then give individual students sentence cards. Invite them to mingle within the class saying their sentences in a particular emotional style and the others have to guess what it is from the intonation used.

Such techniques can help break down the ego boundaries of students and so make them more receptive to undergoing change in their fossilised pronunciation systems.

Activities that involve mingling are an ideal way of getting students out of their chairs and of ensuring movement in the classroom. At the same time they provide an effective way of giving the learners controlled practice in the use of target language. Hand out a copy of one of the worksheets to each member of the class, then invite the students to circulate round the room to find people who have done the things listed. They should make a note of their names and any extra details they can obtain to share with the rest of the group. The **Find Someone Who...!** activities presented on the following pages are designed to practise phrasal verbs.

Find Someone Who...!

Circulate round the room to find people who can answer the following questions. Then make a note of their names and any extra details you can obtain to share with the rest of the group.

1. who has bumped into someone famous (find out who)

2. who could do with a holiday

3. who has recently taken up a new hobby (find out what)

4. whose job gets them down (find out why)

5. who can't get by on the money they earn each week

6. who turned up late for school today (find out why)

7. who has recently broken off a relationship

8. who was brought up by the sea (find out where)

9. who has turned down a marriage proposal

10. who looks up to the Prime Minister (find out why)

11. who has given up smoking

12. who goes in for dangerous sports (find out what)

13. who has passed out in a public place

14. who can take off someone famous (find out who)

15. who puts off going to the dentist

Find Someone Who...!

Circulate round the room to find people who can answer the following questions. Then make a note of their names and any extra details you can obtain to share with the rest of the group.

1. who has been laid off

2. who takes after either of their parents

3. who has been beaten up or knocked out

4. who regularly turns in after midnight

5. who has recently struck up a new relationship

6. who has had their flat/house broken into

7. who can put you up for a couple of nights

8. who has been taken in by a confidence trickster

9. who feels they could settle down in another country

10. who has children to look after

11. who feels they're not cut out for the work they do

12. who has come up against problems while living in England

13. who would like to see the current Government brought down

14. who has recently split up with their partner

15. who finds it difficult to hold down a job

Find Someone Who...!

Circulate round the room to find people who can answer the following questions. Then make a note of their names and any extra details you can obtain to share with the rest of the group.

1. who likes to lie in on Sundays

2. who has come upon a bargain recently (find out what)

3. who would like to see the death penalty done away with

4. who has dropped off in the middle of a lesson

5. who feels they are not cut out for the job they do (find out why)

6. who has got away with a crime (find out what)

7. who has been bowled over by someone recently (find out why)

8. who has botched up an important exam

9. who would like to branch out (find out what they would like to branch out into)

10. who has been ripped off as a tourist on holiday

11. whose back plays them up

12. who has recently been ticked off by their boss/teacher (find out why)

13. who sucks up to their boss

14. who has walked out of a job (find out why)

15. who has recently splashed out on something (find out what)

Find Someone Who...!

Circulate round the room to find people who can answer the following questions. Then make a note of their names and any extra details you can obtain to share with the rest of the group.

1. who knows how to look after babies

2. who has been called on to make a speech

3. who works out regularly in a gym or health club

4. who has been set upon by muggers

5. who would stand by you if you were in trouble

6. who has had their wisdom teeth pulled out

7. who sticks by their promises

8. who has struck up a relationship with a native English speaker

9. who gave up their job to study in the UK

10. who has gone out with someone a lot younger than themselves

11. who will own up to having broken the law (find out how)

12. who has missed out on a golden opportunity (find out what)

13. who finds it difficult to put up with living in a big city (find out why)

14. who has set up their own business (find out what)

15. who is crying out for a change in their lives (find out why)

Find Someone Who...!

Circulate round the room to find people who can answer the following questions. Then make a note of their names and any extra details you can obtain to share with the rest of the group.

1. whom you could turn to if you were in trouble

2. who has fallen for someone a lot older than themselves

3. who keeps up with the latest fashions

4. who has got away with breaking the law (find out how)

5. who feels like dropping out of the course (find out why)

6. who has been (or will be) called up for military service

7. who sometimes has to stand in for their boss (find out when)

8. who has fallen out with someone recently (find out why)

9. who can come up with an easy way of making money (find out what it is)

10. who has recently done up their home

11. whose last holiday turned out to be a disappointment (find out why)

12. who has taken on a position of greater responsibility at work recently (find out what)

13. who finds it difficult to keep out of trouble (find out why)

14. who has nodded off during a lesson (find out who the teacher was!)

15. who has recently taken out a loan (find out what for)

The **Find Someone Who...!** activities presented below were produced for an Elementary level class.

Find Someone Who...!

Circulate round the room to find people who can answer the following questions. Then make a note of their names and any extra details you can obtain to share with the rest of the group.

1. likes getting up early in the morning

2. doesn't like living in London (find out why)

3. likes cooking (find out what)

4. doesn't like watching TV (find out why)

5. doesn't like travelling by plane (find out why)

6. likes skiing (find out where they ski)

7. likes listening to music (find out what kind of music)

8. doesn't like shopping (find out why)

9. likes dancing (find out where they go dancing)

10. doesn't like sunbathing (find out why)

Find Someone Who...!

Circulate round the room to find people who can answer the following questions. Then make a note of their names and any extra details you can obtain to share with the rest of the group.

1. who has been on a skiing holiday (find out where)

2. who has flown in a helicopter

3. who has been on a cruise

4. who has ridden a camel (find out whether it was comfortable or not!)

5. who has been scuba diving

6. who has gone on a camping holiday (find out who with)

7. who has been on a hovercraft

8. who has missed a flight (find out why)

9. who has been searched by a Customs Officer

10. who has lost his/her luggage (find out how)

11. who has flown in a hot-air balloon

12. who has slept in a hammock (find out where)

An ideal way of catering for the kinesthetic intelligence type in class is through the use of role-play. There follows a lesson plan based on a traditional story which contains an example of one such role-play.

1. Is it our duty to look after our parents when they grow old or should they go into an Old People's Home? What normally happens in your country?

    Today's story is a traditional Yiddish tale which takes a humorous look at this difficult problem that many of us will have to face one day.

2. *Narrate the story.*

3. *Pause after the mother bird says* "Ah, you're lying" *for the first time and ask the students to predict what follows.* What do you think the mother bird is going to do next?

4. *Arrange the students in groups of three for a role-play. Student A takes the part of an elderly parent, student B the parent's grown-up daughter, and student C the daughter's husband. The question under discussion is whether the parent should go into an Old People's Home or not. The daughter feels guilty about putting her mother into the Home but her husband feels it would be for the best in view of the old woman's condition.*

Student A: You're a middle-aged woman with two young children and a full-time job. Your elderly mother lives with you and needs a lot of attention. You're finding it increasingly difficult to cope with everything but you feel it's your duty to look after her.

Student B: Your wife is suffering from stress and you're worried about her health. You feel she has too much to cope with and that it would be better if her mother went into a Home where she could be properly looked after.

Student C: You want to live an independent life and don't like the idea of going into a Home. You feel that you still have a valuable role to play and that you can help your daughter to look after her children. You blame your son-in-law for the situation because you think he doesn't like you and that's why he proposed the idea.

A Fable Of A Bird And Her Chicks

Once upon a time a mother bird who had three chicks wanted to cross a river. She put the first one under her wing and started flying across. As she flew she said, 'Tell me, child, when I'm old, will you carry me under your wing the way I'm carrying you now?'

'Of course,' replied the chick. 'What a question!' 'Ah,' said the mother bird, 'you're lying.' With that she let the chick slip, and it fell into the river and drowned.

The mother went back for the second chick, which she took under her wing. Once more as she was flying across the river, she said, 'Tell me, child, when I'm old, will you carry me under your wing the way I'm carrying you now?'

'Of course,' replied the chick. 'What a question!'

'Ah,' said the mother bird, 'you're lying.' With that she let the second chick slip, and it also drowned.

Then the mother went back for the third chick, which she took under her wing. Once more she asked in mid-flight, 'Tell me, child, when I am old, will you carry me under your wing the way I'm carrying you now?'

'No, mother,' replied the third chick. 'How could I? By then I'll have chicks of my own to carry.'

'Ah, my dearest child,' said the mother bird, 'you're the one who tells the truth.' With that she carried the third chick to the other bank of the river.

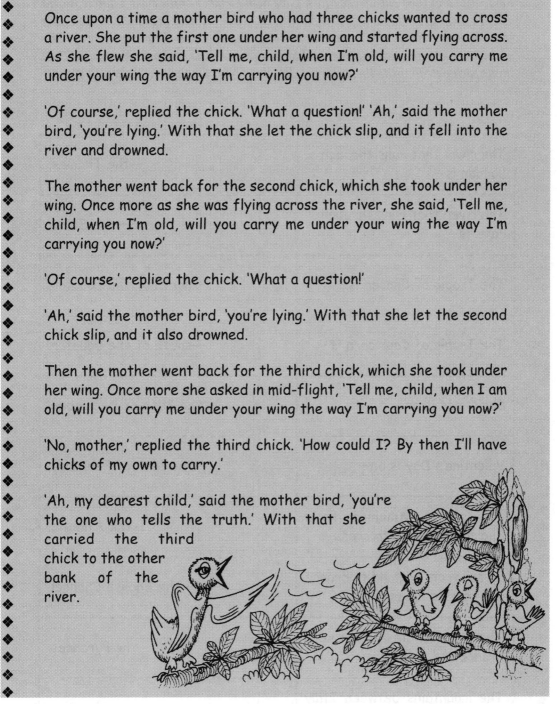

(From *The Second Virago Book Of Fairy Tales"* - Virago Press Ltd, 1992)

❖❖❖❖❖

Not only kinesthetic learners benefit from movement in the classroom. Research indicates that after sitting in one place for about twenty minutes, the brain starts getting starved of oxygen and attention starts to wander. The **Find Your Missing Half** activities presented on the following pages can be used to avoid this problem.

Find Your Missing Half
(fixed expressions with the definite article)

Reproduce and then cut up the cards. Give each member of the class a different card and ask them to circulate to find their missing halves. Encourage them to read their cards to their classmates rather than show them. Once they have found their partners, ask them to sit together and write the rule their sentence illustrates. Then invite each pair to write their rule on the whiteboard for the whole class to see.

The river that runs through London is—	—the Thames.
The river that runs through Paris is—	—the Seine.
The Tropic of Cancer is—	—north of the Equator.
The Tropic of Capricorn is—	—south of the Equator.
Christmas is on—	—the 25th of December.
Valentine's Day is on—	—the 14th of February.
To sail to America from England you have to cross—	—the Atlantic.
To sail from England to France you have to cross—	—the English Channel.
The mountains between France and Spain are—	—the Pyranees.
The mountains between Italy and Switzerland are—	—the Alps.
The longest river in the world is—	—the Mississippi-Missouri.
The largest desert in the world is—	—the Sahara.

The sun—	—rises in the East and sets in the West.
Everyone agrees that the Earth—	—is round but at one time they thought it was flat.
If you like modern art, you should visit—	—the Tate Gallery.
If you're interested in Egyptian mummies, you should visit—	—the British Museum.
When you go to Trafalgar Square, don't forget to visit—	—the National Gallery.
The main concert hall on the South Bank of the river is—	—the Royal Festival Hall.
The Ritz is—	—an elegant five star hotel in Green Park.
The most famous quality newspaper is—	—The Times.
The popular newspaper that has the largest circulation is—	—The Sun.
If you like plays by Shakespeare, you should get tickets for—	—the Globe Theatre.
If you enjoy arias by Mozart and have lots of money, go to—	—the Royal Opera House.
The Prime Minister lives at—	—Number 10 Downing Street.
Buckingham Palace is the home of—	—the Queen.
Britain is one of the few countries in the world where people—	—drive on the left.
Cornwall is a county in—	—the West of England.

Find Your Missing Half
(fixed expressions with the indefinite article)

Reproduce and then cut up the cards. Give each member of the class a different card and ask them to circulate to find their missing halves. Encourage them to read their cards to their classmates rather than show them. Once they have found their partners, invite them to write the fixed expressions on the whiteboard for the whole class to see.

I keep sneezing. I think I've caught—	—a cold.
Your forehead feels hot. I think you've got—	—a temperature.
I've been shouting so much that I've got—	—a sore throat.
I can't wait because I'm in—	—a hurry.
I've left my briefcase on the train. What—	—a nuisance!
I heard you failed the exam. What—	—a pity!
She never loses her temper. She's got—	—a great deal of patience.
It cost next to nothing in a sale. What—	—a bargain!
I was feeling sleepy after lunch so I had—	—a nap.
Did you have—	—a good time at the party last night?
If you want to see a doctor, you'll have to make—	—an appointment.
If you've got—	—a toothache, you'd better go to the dentist.

Find Your Missing Half
(fixed expressions with the zero article)

Reproduce and then cut up the cards. Give each member of the class a different card and ask them to circulate to find their missing halves. Encourage them to read their cards to their classmates rather than show them. Once they have found their partners, invite them to write the expressions on the whiteboard for the whole class to see.

Did you go there for pleasure or—	—on business?
I need your help because I'm—	—in trouble.
What you told me doesn't—	—make sense.
The film star didn't want to be pestered by fans—	—so she travelled in disguise.
He was so depressed that he tried—	—to commit suicide.
The acrobat turned—	—head over heels.
There are certain things you just have to learn—	—by heart.
I managed to get to the station—	—just in time.
As it wasn't very far I decided to go there—	—on foot.
I'm afraid we don't keep that particular brand—	—in stock.
I'm afraid we don't always see—	—eye-to-eye with each other.
By law—	—you're innocent until you're proved guilty.

This section would not be complete without mentioning Educational Kinesiology. This was developed by Paul E. Dennison in the 1970s and uses movement to enhance learning potential. Cross crawl movements (any movements that use the opposite arm and leg) help balance activities on both sides of the brain. Marching on the spot, for example, activates the brain, improves co-ordination, stimulates the flow of lymph, helps memory and concentration, improves performance and increases general well-being. Drawing "lazy eights" can be helpful too – tracing in the air the shape of the number eight lying on its side, starting in the centre and going up and out. It has been found that by carrying out such activities prior to reading/writing tasks, performance can be greatly improved.

Drawing "lazy eights"

Unit 3: How To Cater For Musical Intelligence

First of all, here is a questionnaire for students to complete to find out how musical they are. Learning is more likely to take place when the conscious attention is deflected from the goal, which is how incidental learning occurs. The following activity provides controlled practice in the use of the Present Simple tense with adverbs of frequency but there is no reason why the students need to know this. Their authentic reason for doing the task is to find out more about themselves.

After pre-teaching new vocabulary, arrange the students in groups. Hand out a copy of the questionnaire to an "interviewer" in each group who reads the questions to the other students and takes on the role of the teacher. Only the interviewer should be able to see the copy and (s)he presents the questionnaire to the group as a listening activity. Meanwhile, you can circulate to provide any assistance required. The next stage is for the students to add up their scores and assess the results, which can be examined and discussed by the class as a whole.

1. **How often do people tell you that you've got a good singing voice?**
   a. whenever you sing
   b. occasionally
   c. never

2. **How frequently can you tell when a musical note is off-key?**
   a. always
   b. sometimes
   c. hardly ever

3. **How often do you listen to music on the radio, records, cassettes or compact discs?**
   a. regularly
   b. from time to time
   c. almost never

4. **Do you play a musical instrument?**
   a. yes
   b. no

5. **How important is music to you?**
   a. very
   b. a little
   c. not at all

6. **How often do you sing or hum to yourself?**
   a. frequently
   b. sometimes
   c. never

7. **How easily can you keep time to a piece of music with a simple percussion instrument?**
   a. easily
   b. with difficulty

8. Do you know the tunes to a lot of different songs or musical pieces?
   a. yes
   b. no

9. How frequently do you remember the tunes of songs you like?
   a. always
   b. occasionally
   c. hardly ever

10. How often do you make tapping sounds or sing while working, studying or learning?
    a. frequently
    b. sometimes
    c. probably never

Check Your Score

1.	a-2	b-1	c-0	6. a-2	b-1	c-0
2.	a-2	b-1	c-0	7. a-2	b-0	
3.	a-2	b-1	c-0	8. a-2	b-0	
4.	a-2	b-0		9. a-2	b-1	c-0
5.	a-2	b-1	c-0	10. a-2	b-1	c-0

What Your Score Means:

0-7   I'm afraid you have no musical talent at all – in fact you're a bit of a disaster! Never mind, because you can still enjoy listening to it even if you can't play a musical instrument or sing.

8-14   Although you enjoy music, it doesn't seem to play a major part in your life. It's unlikely that you're ever going to become a famous opera singer or a rock superstar but then you probably don't want to be anyway.

15-20   It's clear that you're an extremely musical person and that you probably play an instrument and/or sing to a high standard. The other students in the class should ask you for your autograph because perhaps you're going to be famous one day!

The use of songs in the classroom is a popular activity, particularly suitable for the end of a heavy working week. A possible danger is overkill, especially if you always deal with songs in the same way. Try to vary your approach and you can then make the activity a regular feature of your programme. To make it more student-centred, let the students choose which songs they would like to cover instead of imposing your own musical tastes.

Three possible approaches are presented below.

A Cloze Test

1. *Global questions to test general comprehension*
2. *Play the song*
3. *Go through the answers*
4. *Hand out the cloze test*
5. *Play the song a second time*
6. *Check the answers*
7. *Sing the song together (optional)*
8. *Discussion of the issues raised*

Spot The Mistakes

1. *Hand out copies of the lyrics with deliberate mistakes*
2. *Play the song for students to mark the corrections*
3. *Check the answers*
4. *Sing the song together*

A Dictation

1. *Pre-questions*
2. *Play the song*
3. *Go through the answers*
4. *Play the song a second time pausing after each line*
5. *Students call out the words and you board them*
6. *If there are any missing words, repeat the process*
7. *Sing the song together*
8. *Follow-up activity (discussion or role-play)*

- Other ways of dealing with songs include giving everyone a card with one of the lines from the lyrics and asking them to arrange themselves in the correct order – ideal for kinesthetic learners to give them an opportunity to have a stretch and to stop them from becoming restless. Another possibility is to cut up the lines, to place them in envelopes, and to ask the students to order them in groups.

- At the end of the term or year, how about a **Name That Song** game? Record a cassette with a couple of lines from each of the songs you have used during the course. Hand out a list of the titles and ask the students to number them according to the order in which they are played. Alternatively, you can devise a matching activity with a list of titles and a list of lines from the lyrics.

- Another possibility is to type out the words of one verse and a chorus from a popular song and to invite the students to rewrite the lyrics on a particular theme. They can then be invited to sing the new versions to each other or in small groups.

The same pre-questions can be used for whatever song you choose and these can be prepared on an OHP sheet.

> Name of the singer?
> Name of the song?
> Any lines you can remember?
> What's the song about?

As an alternative to the pre-questions, the students can be asked to predict what they are likely to hear.

"I'm going to play you a love song, but a love song with a difference. What do you suppose is different or unusual about it? Now listen to the song to find out if your prediction was correct."

Traditional folk songs might not be everyone's cup of tea. However, unlike popular songs they never date and there is a lot you can do with them in the classroom. If you follow a topic-based approach, a song like *Reynardine* can be included under the heading of "Animals", *The Unquiet Grave* could be classified under "The Supernatural", and *The First Time Ever I Saw Your Face* (a contemporary folk song) can be filed under "Relationships". The lyrics for the songs are presented on the following pages, together with possible follow-up activities.

Reynardine

This is a traditional folk song that embodies the legend of the man who can turn himself into a fox – a sort of werewolf. Here the myth is brought into disturbing contrast with reality!

One night upon my rambles, two miles below Fermoy
I met a farmer's daughter all on the mountains high
I said, my pretty fair maid your beauty shines so clear
All on these lonesome mountains I'm glad to meet you here

She said, kind sir be civil, my company forsake
For in my own opinion I fear you are some rake
And if my parents they should know, my life they would destroy
For keeping of your company all on the mountains high

He said, my dear I am no rake brought up in Venus' train
But I'm seeking for concealment all on the lonesome plain
Your beauty so enticed me I could not pass it by
So it's with my gun I'll guard you all on the mountains high

Her cherry cheeks and her ruby lips they lost their former dye
She fainted in his arms there all on the mountains high
They hadn't kissed but once or twice till she came to again
With that she kindly asked him, pray tell to me your name

If by chance you look for me perhaps you'll not me find
For I'll be in my castle – enquire for Reynardine
Sun and dark she followed him, his teeth did brightly shine
And he led her over the mountains, that sly bold Reynardine.

"One night while I was walking in the mountains, I came across a farmer's daughter. I told her how beautiful I thought she was and how happy I was to meet her ..."

Now continue the story in present day English!

The Unquiet Grave

Cold blows the wind to my true love
And gently drops the rain,
I never had but one sweetheart,
And in greenwood she lies slain.
I'll do as much for my sweetheart
As any young man may;
I'll sit and mourn all on her grave
For a twelvemonth and a day.

When the twelvemonth and one day was past,
The ghost began to speak;
'Why sit you here all on my grave,
And will not let me sleep?'
'There's one thing that I want, sweetheart,
There's one thing that I crave;
And that is a kiss from your lily-white lips
Then I'll go from your grave.'

'My breast it is as cold as clay,
My breath smells earthly strong;
And if you kiss my cold clay lips,
Your days they won't be long.
Go fetch me water from the desert,
And blood from out of a stone;
Go fetch me milk from a fair maid's breast
That a young man never has known.'

'Oh down in yonder grove, sweetheart,
Where you and I would walk,
The first flower that ever I saw
Is withered to a stalk.
The stalk is withered and dry, sweetheart,
And the flower will never return;
And since I lost my own sweetheart,
What can I do but mourn?

'When shall we meet again, sweetheart?
When shall we meet again?'
'When the oaken leaves that fall from the trees
Are green and spring up again.
Are green and spring up again, sweetheart,
Are green and spring up again,
When the oaken leaves that fall from the trees
Are green and spring up again.'

This is a traditional ballad about coming to terms with death. The comfort offered to the young man is the cycle of life, which is seen in the oak in the final verse.

"The ghost asked the young man why he sat on her grave and would not let her sleep. He replied that there was one thing he wanted more than anything else ..."

Now report the rest of the dialogue!

"The First Time Ever I Saw Your Face" by Ewan MacColl
(with deliberate mistakes)

The first time ever I slapped your face
I saw your gun rise with surprise
And the moon and the stars were the gift you gave
To the park and plenty of flies my love
To the park and plenty of flies

The first time ever I knocked you out
I felt the pain shoot through my hand
Like the trembling heart of a captive bird
That was slaughtered on demand my love
That was slaughtered on demand

The first time ever I danced with you
And felt your big feet tread on mine
I thought our joy would cost the earth
And pass with a friend of mine my love
And pass with a friend of mine

"The First Time Ever I Saw Your Face" by Ewan MacColl
(correct lyrics)

The first time ever I saw your face
I thought the sun rose in your eyes
And the moon and the stars were the gift you gave
To the dark and empty skies my love
To the dark and empty skies

The first time ever I kissed your mouth
I felt the earth move in my hand
Like the trembling heart of a captive bird
That was there at my command my love
That was there at my command

The first time ever I lay with you
And felt your heartbeat cover mine
I thought our joy would fill the earth
And last till the end of time my love
And last till the end of time

Now prepare an account of and/or write a description of "The First Time" you did something special to present to the rest of the class. It could be about the first time you met a partner, real or imaginary, or the first time you did something new.

At the other end of the spectrum, songs like **Ten Green Bottles** can be used for teaching numbers. The possibilities for using songs in the classroom are limitless - all you need is a little imagination. And if you can play the guitar and sing to the class, then so much the better.

Music can also be used for work on phonology. Passages of staccato and legato character can be juxtaposed to illustrate the discrepancy between no linking and smooth linking of sounds. The contrast could be illustrated by playing the Third Movement of Mozart's Horn Concerto No. 4 and then the Second Movement of the Horn Concerto No. 3 . The technique can also be adapted to practise difficult sounds, eg "la, la" (staccato) or humming (legato). A fun way of working on intonation is to provide learners with kazoos to imitate the patterns.

People are most receptive to right-brain insights when the body is relaxed and the mind free from internal chatter. Moreover, brain research confirms that as stress increases, the ability to learn decreases, so establishing the right kind of atmosphere in the classroom is clearly crucial. The learner under stress will resort to rote and ritualistic responses, or "flight or fight" responses, and be resistant to anything new. ("Flight or fight" is the term used to describe the physiological changes that take place under stress) In other words, a learner who is under stress will not learn anything as it's biologically impossible! Making use of music in the classroom can help create optimal learning conditions in which the students feel relaxed and so produce their best possible work.

Teachers frequently give instructions for a particular activity and then tell the class that they have a certain number of minutes in which to complete it. Why? This only puts unnecessary pressure on the group. An alternative is to play background music during the task, then to turn up the volume before fading it to indicate that the time has come to finish. Surely this is preferable to having to bang on the table, clap your hands or shout to gain their attention. Music can also be used to promote the students' self-esteem: try playing a fanfare to greet them when they walk into the room for class, or recording a burst of applause to play each time they produce a correct response.

Another way of using songs or music can be to set the scene, for the Presentation stage in the Suggestopedic cycle, for example. Suggestopedia originated with the work of Dr Lozanov, a Bulgarian psychotherapist in the 1970s. It entails the creation of an optimum learning state by removing barriers to learning and providing a positive expectation of success. The four-phase cycle consists of the Presentation, the Active Concert – the target material read to classical music, the Passive Concert – the target material read to Baroque music, and the Activation. The purpose of the Presentation is to give a lively overview and to connect the "known" to the "target" material. Although the Suggestopedic approach has proved to be an effective way of teaching languages, it is controversial and clearly not everyone's cup of tea. However, the first stage of the cycle can be incorporated into more conventional teaching models without causing too much of a shock to the system!

For a Suggestopedic lesson, the classroom would be prepared before the students arrive – the walls would be covered with visuals related to the content of the lesson, music would be playing related to the target material, and the table covered with realia dealing with the content of the lesson. The students walk into the classroom and pick up the objects from the table and start talking about them. The lesson could be about holidays, for example. You could cover the walls with travel posters, play the sound of waves breaking on a beach, and have a suitcase full of holiday items and souvenirs placed on the table. This will create a memorable learning experience that they are unlikely to forget.

The Baroque music that Dr Lozanov recommends for the Passive Concert in the Suggestopedic cycle includes *Concerti Grossi*, Op. 6, No. 4, 10, 11, 12 by Corelli and *Five Concerti for Flute and Chamber Orchestra* (G Major, F Major, G Minor, C Major) by Vivaldi. The beat per second paces the brain into a slower frequency alpha range of seven to eleven cycles per second.

Unit 4: How To Cater For Interpersonal Intelligence

Whenever you introduce pair or groupwork into the classroom, you cater for the interpersonal intelligence type. However, unless you vary these forms of interaction, the students may well find themselves always working with the same people. Try to avoid a pairwork activity followed by another pairwork activity unless the learners change partners in between.

The students themselves occasionally react negatively to pairwork, saying they do not want to be exposed to poor models of spoken English. In such cases it is worth pointing out that when they leave the classroom to enter the real world outside, it is more than likely that most of their communication in English will be with other non-native speakers. For this reason it is just as important for them to be able to understand a German or a Japanese person speaking English as a native speaker of the language. The other justification for pair or groupwork is that it increases the opportunity for Student Talking Time. This may seem obvious to us as teachers but it is still worth mentioning in class, as not all the learners will necessarily be aware of this.

It never ceases to amaze me that students can work side by side together for months without learning each others' names! One way of dealing with this problem is to nominate a particular student to answer a question, then for this same student to choose one of his/her peers to answer the next one. In this way they are obliged to learn the names of their classmates. It is also a less teacher-centred way of checking the answers to an exercise you have set the class to complete.

Forcing students to work in pairs or groups can be just as damaging as not providing an opportunity for this form of interaction. It is necessary to take into account the learners' preferred behaviour patterns or metaprograms. Metaprograms are the non-conscious filters our brain habitually uses to select relevant information from our sensory experience. They derive from Robert Bailey's *Language and Behaviour (LAB) Profile* created in the early 1980s, which in turn was based on ideas from Neuro-Linguistic Programming. Bailey reduced the original sixty patterns to fourteen and developed specific questions to determine each metaprogram. For example, one of the patterns refers to style. Twenty percent of the population prefer working alone without interruption and like control and

responsibility; twenty percent are co-operative and like sharing responsibility as part of a team; and sixty percent enjoy both. Imposing pairwork on students who prefer working alone, according to this model, can only be counter-productive.

Students with highly developed interpersonal intelligence enjoy collaborative learning and have the ability to enter into the "map" of another, to make sense of the world from another's viewpoint. Some examples of activities that give learners the opportunity to make use of this talent are presented below. (Gardner set out to establish that intelligence is not something fixed, and uses the words "talent" and "intelligence" interchangeably.)

Pairwork interviews are particularly suitable for the first day with a new class as they promote plenty of Student Talking Time. They also give you an opportunity to assess the level of the class, their strengths and weaknesses, while taking a back seat. If you are new to the class but the students have been together as a group for some time, there is no point in asking them to find out basic information about each other because they will already know this. The questions presented below are designed to ensure that this is not a problem as the students are very unlikely to know what their classmates' answers will be! The questions have been taken from interviews with celebrities in the colour supplements of the Sunday newspapers. When teaching larger classes, you can invite the students to form circles of eight for the feedback stage and you can move from group to group to monitor the process. If you feel that the students are suspicious of you and perhaps mistrustful of your eligibility to be their teacher, you can make a note of errors that crop up while monitoring on an OHT.

You can then flash this up at the end of the session and invite them to self-correct. This should serve the purpose of proving to the class that "you know your stuff", so inspiring their confidence in you! The activity is suitable for students of Intermediate level and above.

Work in pairs. Choose five questions from the list below to ask your partner, then report back to the rest of the class with your findings.

- What single thing would most improve the quality of your life?
- What is your greatest regret?
- What are you reading at present?
- When and where were you happiest?
- Who are your favourite musicians?
- Who or what is the greatest love of your life?
- What is the trait you most deplore in others?
- If you could buy anything you wanted, what would you choose?
- Where would you love to go on holiday, and why?
- Which living person do you most despise?

◆◆◆◆◆

- What is your idea of perfect happiness?
- Which living person do you most admire, and why?
- Which trait do you most deplore in others?
- On what occasions do you lie?
- What objects do you always carry with you?
- Who are your favourite writers?
- Which talent would you most like to have, and why?
- What is your greatest fear?
- How would you like to be remembered when you die?
- What is your greatest extravagance?

◆◆◆◆◆

- ◆ Which historical figure do you most identify with, and why?
- ◆ What has been your most embarrassing moment?
- ◆ What single thing would improve the quality of your life?
- ◆ What do you most dislike about your appearance?
- ◆ What is your most unappealing habit?
- ◆ What is your favourite smell?
- ◆ What makes you depressed?
- ◆ Which living person do you most admire, and why?
- ◆ What keeps you awake at night?
- ◆ What is the most important lesson life has taught you?

◆◆◆◆◆

An alternative to the first day activity presented above is a class survey in which the students can mingle. Below are some questions. Cut them up and give each member of the class one. Ask the students to go round the class and collect the answers to the question, making a note of who said what. When finished, go over the answers together.

- ◆ What kind of TV programmes do you like?
- ◆ If you won £1,000, what would you buy?
- ◆ What makes you laugh the most?
- ◆ What makes you happy?
- ◆ What lie have you told recently?
- ◆ When did you last feel scared?
- ◆ What embarrasses you?
- ◆ What subject did you most enjoy at school?
- ◆ Who would you most like to spend an evening with, and why?
- ◆ What is your favourite food?
- ◆ What is your favourite smell?
- ◆ Who is your favourite film star?
- ◆ What makes you feel sad?
- ◆ If you could be someone else, who would you want to be?
- ◆ What time of day do you like most, and why?
- ◆ What job would you most like to do, and why?

◆◆◆◆◆

Collective dialogue-writing is another way of providing an opportunity to cater for interpersonal intelligence. The following set of activities was designed for an Advanced level class to improve their mastery of the use of the articles by focusing on fixed expressions with the zero article, with the indefinite article, and with the definite article.

Go through the fixed expressions with the class, column by column, to make sure they are understood. Arrange the students in pairs or groups. Ask them to select five of the expressions and incorporate them into a dialogue. Then invite the students to act out their dialogues for the rest of the class.

Food & Drink

zero article	the indefinite article	the definite article
to go shopping	to go on a diet	to pay/foot the bill
to lose/put on weight	to have a snack/drink	to ask for the bill
to eat between meals	to book a table for two	to split the bill
to have breakfast in bed	to have a bite to eat	to do the cooking
to have dinner by candlelight	to be as drunk as a lord	to do the washing-up
to have tea with milk/sugar	to be as sober as a judge	to do the drying
to have lunch/supper	to be as greedy as a pig	to lay the table
service is included	I could eat a horse!	the dish of the day
to drink alcohol with ice/lemon	to try a mouthful	to keep the change
	to go on a picnic	the set menu
	to drink a toast to someone	whisky on the rocks
	to have half a pint/a double	

Travelling

zero article	the indefinite article	the definite article
by train/boat/plane	to be in a hurry/rush	round-the-world
on foot	to come to a standstill	to see the sights
to go sightseeing	to have a good trip	the rush hour
to go camping/skiing	to have a safe flight/journey	I had the time of my life!
to go on business/for pleasure	to go on a working holiday	to lie in the sun
to travel first/business class	to go for a swim	the Arrivals Hall
to go abroad	to go away for a weekend break	the Departure Lounge
half-/full-board		the average temperature
to book in advance	to have a complete rest	to drive on the left
from Platform 13/from Gate 8	to go on a cruise	the height of the season
to take out travel insurance	only a five-minute walk	to catch/miss the last bus
to arrive in/on time	as red as a beetroot	take the ... turning on
to set sail for	to have a holiday romance	the left/right
to go through Customs		
to get sunstroke		

Work

zero article	the indefinite article	the definite article
to go on strike	£ ... a month/year	to be on the dole
to be out of work	to make a good impression	to be paid by the hour
on business	to make more of an effort	to get the sack
at/off work	to be (stuck) in a rut	to work your fingers to the bone
to do/work overtime	to have a nine-to-five job	
to be on/off duty	to have a talent/flair for	to do the dirty work
to have job security	to have a dead-end job	the unemployed
to give someone notice	to work like a slave	to reach the top
to be in charge of	to type ... words a minute	to get the hang of something
to have no free time	to make an early start	to rub someone up
to get down to work	to have a good working relationship	the wrong way
to be computer literate		
to have good interpersonal skills		

Health & Medicine

zero article	the indefinite article	the definite article
to have flu/indigestion	to have/catch a cold	to feel under the weather
on prescription	to go on a diet	what's the matter?
to lose weight	to have a toothache/back ache	what seems to be the problem?
to suffer from depression	to ask for a second opinion	to be on the mend
to be in pain	three times a day	to be over the worst
to be in good/safe hands	to have a temperature	to be on the road to recovery
to suffer from shock	to have a headache	to have the hiccups
to be in a coma	to be given a clean bill of health	to be out of the woods
to lose consciousness	to have an upset stomach	to have one foot in the grave
to regain consciousness	to be as fit as a fiddle	over the counter
to be out of danger		
to have diarrhoea		
to have constipation		
to buy drugs/medicine		

Brainstorming is also an effective way of catering for interpersonal intelligence. It can either be done informally or in a more systematic way. You can write the subject for discussion on the board and invite the students to come up with suggestions or you can provide them with a set of leading questions in order to generate ideas. The suggestions can be boarded in a non-linear format – in the form of a spidergram, for example. Instead of holding centre stage yourself, you can invite one of the students to the front to do the boarding while you take a back seat. The set of leading questions presented below were adapted from the book *Process Writing* by Ron White & Valerie Arndt (1991) and are designed to generate ideas on the subject of battery hens. However, the same set of questions can be applied to any topic for discussion.

- What is the colour, size, shape, feel, smell, sound of battery hens?
- What are battery hens like or unlike?
- What do battery hens bring to mind?
- What are battery hens part of?
- What can be done with battery hens?
- What points can be put for and against battery hens?

Games requiring teamwork are an ideal vehicle to cater for interpersonal intelligence too. Students need to concentrate more on the rules and objectives of games than on the grammar structures and vocabulary needed to play them. For this reason, new material is perceived in an indirect way and according to research by Dr Lozanov, the Bulgarian psychotherapist responsible for developing the Suggestopedic approach, what people experience indirectly is retained more easily by long term memory than what they see and hear consciously. Another reason for playing games in the classroom is for the variety they introduce. Not only do they help to hold the student's attention, but they also provide a memorable learning experience which is more likely to leave a lasting impression. However, perhaps the most important reason of all for playing games is that they help to make language learning fun!

Language noughts and crosses is played with two teams, exactly like ordinary noughts and crosses, except that the teams have to answer a question correctly before they can put their O or X in the grid. If they answer incorrectly, the other team has the opportunity of answering and, if correct, they place their O or X in the square of their choice. The questions can be aimed at individual members of the team or the team as a whole. The players can pick a subject to answer from the five different categories provided. The game is particularly suitable for Friday afternoons as it can be used to recycle all the work covered during the week. Two sample games for Intermediate level students are presented below.

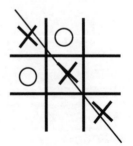

Game 1 (Elementary)

Where Do They Work?

a. a librarian

b. a nurse

c. a chef

d. a farmer

e. a clown

f. a chambermaid

g. a dentist

h. a mechanic

i. a professor

j. a diplomat

Opposites. What's the opposite of...?

a. dangerous

b. asleep

c. empty

d. noisy

e. interesting

f. strong

g. married

h. beautiful

i. absent

j. rude

You Have 30 Seconds To Give Me ... Starting From Now!

a. the twelve months of the year

b. six forms of transport

c. the seven days of the week

d. six pieces of furniture

e. the names of eight different animals

f. six subjects children can study at school

g. the names of six different vegetables

h. eight parts of the body

i. the names of six different types of fruit

j. eight items of clothing/things people wear

Who Uses It?

a. a blackboard

b. a stethoscope

c. handcuffs

d. a camera

e. a tractor

f. a typewriter

g. a drill

h. an apron

i. a tray

j. a sewing machine

Words Confused & Words Misused. Explain the differences:

a. their/there

b. say/tell

c. who's/whose

d. bring/take

e. fair/fare

f. look at/watch

g. weak/week

h. high/tall

i. knows/nose

j. a relation/a relationship

Game 2 (Elementary)

Plurals. What's the plural of...?

a. tooth
b. child
c. shelf
d. son-in-law
e. mouse
f. sheep
g. thief
h. foot
i. mother-in-law
j. person

Numbers

a. How many players are there in a football team?
b. How many weeks are there in a year?
c. How many fingers have you got?
d. How many years are there in a century?
e. How many are there in a dozen?
f. How many toes have you got?
g. How many days are there in a leap year?
h. How many years are there in a decade?
i. What's the population of London?
j. How many sides has a triangle got?

Words Confused & Words Misused. Explain the differences:

a. pair/pear
b. borrow/lend
c. to/too
d. hear/listen
e. cook/cooker
f. quiet/quite
g. game/play
h. wear/where
i. foreigner/stranger
j. peace/piece

Prepositions. Find the missing prepositions:

a. Thank you ... all your help.
b. Do you agree ... me?
c. I like listening ... classical music.
d. She lives ... her own.
e. He got married ... one of his students.
f. You can borrow books ... a library.
g. What's the matter ... you?
h. Do you believe ... God?
i. You shouldn't steal. It's ... the law.
j. I'm interested ... collecting stamps.

Opposites. Add the correct prefix to make the opposite:

a. usual
b. correct
c. possible
d. legal
e. dependent
f. agree
g. capable
h. understand
i. pleased
j. practical

Game 3 (Elementary)

Family Tree

a. The parents of my mother are my ... .
b. The son of my father is my ... .
c. The sister of my mother is my ... .
d. The son of my brother is my ... .
e. The children of my father's brother are my ... .
f. The daughter of my sister is my ... .
g. The woman I'm married to is my ... .
h. The father of my wife is my ... .
i. The man my mother married after my father died is my ... .
j. The sister of my wife is my ... .

Pairs. Find the missing word to complete the pair:

a. more or ...
b. salt and ...
c. sooner or ...
d. fish and ...
e. bed and ...
f. oil and ...
g. husband and ...
h. rock and ...
i. bride and ...
j. country and ...

Where Was It Said?

a. Take off your clothes, please. I'd like to examine you.
b. Waiter, can I have the bill please?
c. Smile, please. Say "cheese"!
d. Could I try them on to see if they fit?
e. Could you check the oil, please?
f. Have you got anything to declare?
g. Could I have a paying-in slip, please?
h. I can't sell them to you without a prescription.
i. Five first-class stamps, please.
j. Have you got a single room for the night?

Opposites. What's the opposite of ...?

a. true
b. cloudy
c. clean
d. bored
e. tight
f. wide
g. careful
h. innocent
i. ill
j. sweet

Spot The Mistake

a. Would you like dancing with me?
b. The teacher got married with one of his students.
c. If you've got a headache, you should to take an aspirin.
d. What kind of music do you like listening?
e. I was an English teacher since I left University.
f. When you went on holiday, how was the weather?
g. How many money do you earn each month?
h. I think learning English is easy. Are you agree with me?
i. I haven't got any money. Can you borrow me some?
j. The book you're studying is the same than mine.

Game 4 (Elementary)

Where Can You Buy Them?

a. stamps
b   fruit and vegetable
c. meat
d. bread and cakes
e. fish

f. a package holiday
g. a book
h. paper and envelopes
i. a bottle of aspirin
j. a hammer and nails

Spot The Mistake

a. How many years have you?
b. Don't forget to make your homework tonight!
c. I like your new dress - it looks very well.
d. You come from Spain, aren't you?
e. Would you like going out for dinner with me?
f. She's usually drinking tea for breakfast.
g. I'm afraid I don't know nothing about computers.
h. Studying English costs a lot of money, isn't it?
i. He likes very much the school. He's very pleased with it.
j. If you want to lose weight, you don't have to eat sweets and chocolates.

Words Confused & Words Misused. Explain the differences:

a. meat/meet
b. a living room/a dining room
c. hear/here
d. a few/a little
e. fall/feel

f. an anniversary/ a birthday
g. interested/interesting
h. a bus/a coach
i. right/write
j. a high school/a secondary school

Prepositions. Find the missing prepositions:

a. Who were you dancing...last night?
b. If you want to lose weight, you should go...a diet.
c. I'm worried...my exam results.
d. Why were you absent...school yesterday?
e. Foreigners often complain...the English weather.
f. If the weather's good, we can go...a walk.
g. Are you pleased...the progress you've made?
h. I live very near my office so I usually go to work...foot.
i. Why are you so angry...me? What have I done to upset you?
j. If you're short...money, I can lend you some.

Make The Questions From The Answers

a. I'm a teacher.
b. I'm 46 years old.
c. No, I'm single.
d. I'm a typical Leo.
e. I live in Kilburn, in the North of London.
f. I like going to the cinema and meeting my friends.
g. I started working in this school about three years ago.
h. I've been a teacher for twenty five years.
i. When I finish work tonight, I'm going to take a friend out to dinner.
j. If I wasn't a teacher, I'd like to be a rock star.

Game 1 (Intermediate)

Phrasal Verbs
1. I'm sorry I'm late but I was held ... by the traffic.
2. Put the medicine somewhere safe where the children can't get ... it.
3. Please stop worrying because everything will turn ... all right in the end.
4. The value of my flat has gone ... since I bought it because of the recession.
5. A lot of research has been carried ... into the causes of cancer.
6. It's not easy to bring ... children when you're a single parent.
7. As I've got nowhere to stay, could you put me ... for a couple of nights?
8. If you still don't understand what to do, I'll go ... the instructions again.
9. I hope I can depend on you and that you won't let me ... .
10. When my son grows ... , he wants to be a doctor.

Abbreviations. What do these abbreviations stand for?
1. V.I.P.   4. p.a.   7. M.P.   10. R.S.V.P.
2. m.p.h.   5. U.K.   8. s.a.e.
3. E.U.   6. a/c   9. Ph.D.

Opposites. Make the opposites by adding a prefix:
1. correct   6. balanced
2. honest   7. complete
3. perfect   8. probable
4. responsible   9. manage
5. understand   10. European

General Knowledge
1. How many wives did King Henry VIII have?
2. Who is the head of the Church of England?
3. Where can you see men wearing kilts?
4. What happened in 1066?
5. Where in Scotland is there supposed to be a monster?
6. Where in London can you find models made of wax?
7. What's the name of the Queen's husband?
8. How old do you have to be to get married without your parents' consent?
9. Which museum in London is named after a Queen and her husband?
10. Who was Oliver Cromwell?

Numbers. Find the missing numbers:
1. How many days are there in a fortnight?
2. How many lives is a cat supposed to have?
3. How many days are there in a Leap Year?
4. ... swallow doesn't make a summer.
5. ... heads are better than one.
6. A teenager is a person between the ages of ... and ... .
7. You can celebrate your silver wedding anniversary when you've been married for ... years.
8. It takes ... to make a quarrel.
9. A stitch in time saves ... .
10. It's difficult to say whose fault it is – it's ... of one and half a dozen of the other.

Game 2 (Intermediate)

Phrasal Verbs

1. I had to come by bus because my car broke ... .
2. Is it an informal party or do I need to dress ... ?
3. You're not as young as you used to be. It's time you got married and settled ... .
4. Have you fixed ... where you're going on holiday yet?
5. I don't understand what's going ... here.
6. The magazine *Time Out* comes ... every Tuesday.
7. If you've run ... of money, I can lend you some.
8. Have you ever thought ... working overseas?
9. The teacher asked one of the students to hand ... the books to the class.
10. They asked me to fill ... an application form when I went for the interview.

Abbreviations

1. P.T.O
2. Ltd.
3. U.N.O.
4. w.p.m.
5. G.B.
6. St.
7. P.S.
8. W.H.O.
9. M.Sc.
10. G.P.

Opposites

1. efficient
2. comfort
3. patient
4. regular
5. pronounce
6. reliable
7. tolerant
8. personal
9. informed
10. smoker

General Knowledge

1. Where can you find the statue of Eros?
2. Name three of the five London airports.
3. Where does the Prime Minister live?
4. Who designed St Paul's Cathedral?
5. Where can you find London Zoo?
6. What's the name of the evening newspaper in London?
7. Name two Royal residences.
8. Where can you find Egyptian mummies in London?
9. What disaster happened in 1666?
10. Where can you see the Changing of the Guard?

Colours

1. As ... as grass
2. If you mix red and blue, you get ... .
3. As ... as snow
4. The police managed to catch the robbers ...-handed.
5. To be a good gardener, you need to have ... fingers.
6. A ... film is a pornographic one.
7. When someone appears unexpectedly, they arrive out of the ... .
8. What colour do people turn when they blush?
9. It's usual for mourners to be dressed in ... .
10. If you're feeling ..., it's probably because you're depressed.

Game 3 (Intermediate)

Phrasal Verbs
1. I wonder what went wrong and why their marriage broke ... .
2. It's an urgent matter and you should deal ... it as soon as possible.
3. I've been given so much work to do that I'll never get ... it all.
4. If you don't attend school regularly, you won't keep ... with the rest of the class.
5. If you put ... going to the dentist, your toothache will only get worse.
6. Can you do ... the back of my dress, please?
7. When the price of property comes ..., we hope to be able to buy a home of our own.
8. I was hoping to get the job but unfortunately they turned me ... .
9. I can't put ... with your disgusting behaviour any longer and I never want to see you again.
10. I hope I can count ... you to arrive on time.

Abbreviations
1. U.F.O.   4. etc.   7. Dr   10. E.F.L.
2. Dept.   5. U.S.A.   8. I.M.F.
3. N.H.S.   6. Sq.   9. B.A.

Opposites
1. convenient   6. forgettable
2. advantage   7. direct (adjective)
3. practical   8. moral
4. literate   9. fiction
5. calculate   10. legible

General Knowledge
1. What's the capital of Scotland?
2. Where was Shakespeare born?
3. How many players are there in a cricket team?
4. What does the United Kingdom consist of?
5. Which English Queen never got married?
6. What's the largest football stadium in London?
7. Who is the Prince of Wales?
8. How old do you have to be before you can vote?
9. Which two teams take part in a boatrace each year on the Thames?
10. Who was Guy Fawkes?

Parts Of The Body. Find the missing parts of the body:
1. I hope you pass the exam and I'll keep my ... crossed for you.
2. To be a good gardener, you need to have green ... .
3. If you like sweets and chocolates, then you've got a sweet ... .
4. You'll have to learn these irregular verbs by ... .
5. The joint between your leg and your foot is your ... .
6. The joint between your hand and your arm is your ... .
7. Which part of you is supposed to go to heaven after you die?
8. Which finger do you wear a wedding ring on?
9. If you're bald, then you've got no ... .
10. You're getting on my nerves and I'll be glad to see the ... of you.

Game 4 (Intermediate)

Phrasal Verbs

1. You should try ... the trousers before you buy them to see if they fit.
2. Will you look ... my cat for me while I'm on holiday?
3. If you don't know the meaning of a word, you can look it ... in your dictionary.
4. If you turn ... late, then we'll have to leave without you.
5. If you carry ... smoking, you'll damage your health.
6. A lot of innocent people were injured when the bomb went ... .
7. What does the abbreviation BBC stand ... ?
8. Is it a true story or did you make it ... ?
9. They kept arguing with each other so they decided to split ... .
10. I'd like to get ... for a few days and to have a break from work.

Abbreviations

1. BBC	4. Co.	7. P.M.	10. P.R.
2. e.g.	5. C.I.S.	8. a.s.a.p.	
3. V.A.T.	6. i.e.	9. Dip.Ed.	

Opposites

1. expensive	6. familiar
2. approve	7. sincere
3. polite	8. modest
4. legal	9. agree
5. spell	10. sense

General Knowledge

1. Name the two Houses of Parliament.
2. Where can you find the statue of Lord Nelson?
3. What disaster happened in 1665?
4. Where can you find the Crown Jewels?
5. Name the three main political parties.
6. Where can you find Speakers' Corner?
7. Which is the most popular daily newspaper?
8. Who will be the next King or Queen of England?
9. What was the name of the only woman Prime Minister?
10. Where can you stand with one foot on either side of the world?

Animals. Find the missing animals:

1. To swim like a ... .
2. A baby cat is called a ... .
3. If you're a greedy person, then you probably eat like a ... .
4. A baby sheep is called a ... .
5. A doctor for animals is called a ... .
6. Don't look a gift ... in the mouth.
7. As brave as a ... .
8. A ... cannot change its spots.
9. A baby dog is called a ... .
10. As free as a ... .

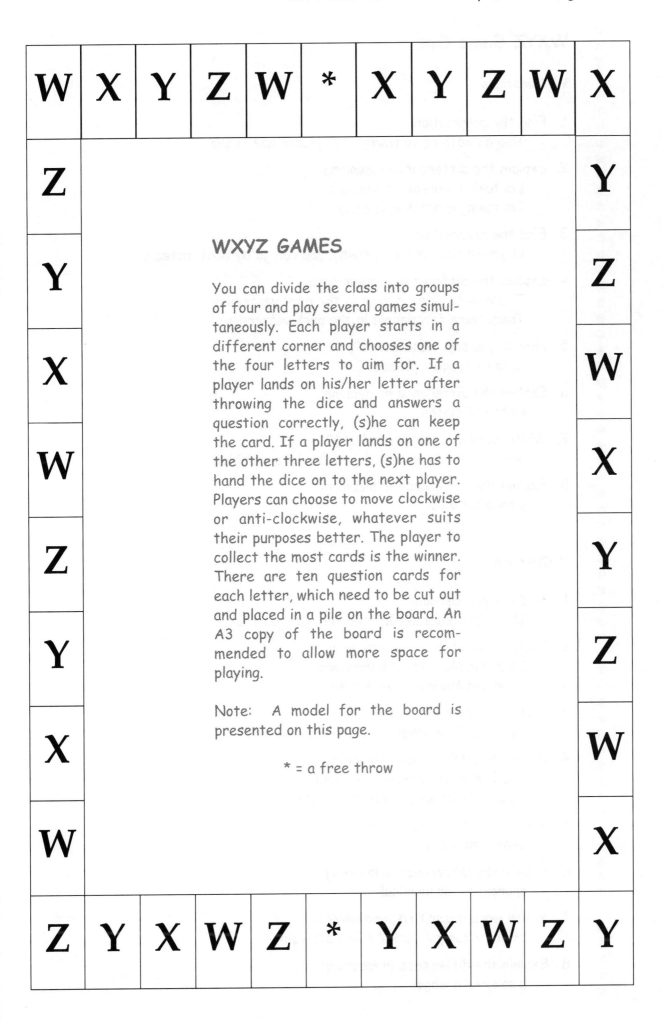

WXYZ GAMES

You can divide the class into groups of four and play several games simultaneously. Each player starts in a different corner and chooses one of the four letters to aim for. If a player lands on his/her letter after throwing the dice and answers a question correctly, (s)he can keep the card. If a player lands on one of the other three letters, (s)he has to hand the dice on to the next player. Players can choose to move clockwise or anti-clockwise, whatever suits their purposes better. The player to collect the most cards is the winner. There are ten question cards for each letter, which need to be cut out and placed in a pile on the board. An A3 copy of the board is recommended to allow more space for playing.

Note: A model for the board is presented on this page.

* = a free throw

WXYZ Game One

W Questions

1. Find the preposition:
    There's nothing to worry ... so please keep calm.

2. Explain the difference in meaning:
    I'm taking a break at present.
    I'm taking a break presently.

3. Find the preposition:
    If you're frightened ... flying, you can go by boat instead.

4. Explain the difference in meaning:
    There were a few people in the park yesterday.
    There were few people in the park yesterday.

5. How do you say these words?
    dough / tough / plough

6. Explain the difference in meaning:
    clothes / cloths

7. Which word doesn't fit, and why?
    boiled / fried / poached / roasted / scrambled

8. Explain the difference in meaning:
    a couple / a pair

X Questions

1. Find the preposition:
    If you subtract seven ... eleven, you get four.

2. Explain the difference in meaning:
    John and Mary love themselves.
    John and Mary love each other.

3. Find the preposition:
    You should be ashamed ... the way you behaved.

4. Explain the difference in meaning:
    I spilt a glass of beer over John.
    I poured a glass of beer over John.

5. How do you say these words?
    debt / mortgage

6. Explain the difference in meaning:
    economic / economical

7. Which word doesn't fit, and why?
    bright / curly / dark / fair / straight

8. Explain the difference in meaning:
    a salary / a wage

Y Questions

1. Find the preposition:
   You shouldn't mix business ... pleasure.

2. Explain the difference in meaning:
   The patient's got a fever.
   The patient's got a temperature.

3. Find the preposition:
   The Prime Minister was criticised ... failing to reduce unemployment.

4. Explain the difference in meaning:
   It's time to start work.
   It's time you started work.

5. How do you say these words?
   bald / bold

6. Explain the difference in meaning:
   let / rent

7. Which word doesn't fit, and why?
   debt / doubt / honest / hotel / island

8. Explain the difference in meaning:
   an artist / a painter

Z Questions

1. Find the preposition:
   Why are you so pessimistic ... the future?

2. Explain the difference in meaning:
   He works as a teacher.
   He works like a slave.

3. Find the preposition:
   If you're keen ... classical music, why don't we go to a concert together?

4. Explain the difference in meaning:
   She was wearing an evening dress when I saw her.
   She was wearing a nightdress when I saw her.

5. How do you say these words?
   photograph / photographer

6. Explain the difference in meaning:
   pour / spill

7. Which word doesn't fit, and why?
   advice / furniture / information / job / money

8. Explain the difference in meaning:
   a package / a packet

WXYZ Game Two

W Questions

1. Find the preposition:
   Why were you absent ... school yesterday?

2. Explain the difference in meaning:
   Did you enjoy the play?
   Did you enjoy the game?

3. Find the preposition:
   The driver was arrested ... breaking the speed limit.

4. Explain the difference in meaning:
   I cut my hair last week.
   I had my hair cut last week.

5. How do you say these words?
   a record (the noun) / to record (the verb)

6. Explain the difference in meaning:
   a bath / a bathe

7. Which word doesn't fit, and why?
   chrome / dome / home / Rome / some

8. Explain the difference in meaning:
   a client / a customer

X Questions

1. Find the preposition:
   The dancers were dressed ... traditional costumes.

2. Explain the difference in meaning:
   He was drunk when he went to the party.
   He got drunk when he went to the party.

3. Find the preposition:
   Foreigners are always complaining ... English food and weather.

4. Explain the difference in meaning:
   She has a shower in her bathroom.
   She's having a shower in her bathroom.

5. How do you say these words?
   separate (the adjective) / separate (the verb)

6. Explain the difference in meaning:
   among / between

7. Which word doesn't fit, and why?
   a duo / a triplet / a quartet / a quintet / a sextet

8. Explain the difference in meaning:
   a note / a notice

Y Questions

1. Find the preposition:
   Are you aware ... how dangerous smoking is?

2. Explain the difference in meaning:
   Have you heard from your friend yet?
   Have you heard about your friend yet?

3. Find the preposition:
   People who suffer ... vertigo can't stand heights.

4. Explain the difference in meaning:
   Why did she go to prison?
   Why did she go to the prison?

5. How do you say these words?
   advertise / advertisement

6. Explain the difference in meaning:
   noisy / nosey

7. Which word doesn't fit, and why?
   January / March / June / October / December

8. Explain the difference in meaning:
   a law / a rule

Z Questions

1. Find the preposition:
   When you speak quickly, I have difficulty ... understanding you.

2. Explain the difference in meaning:
   The police found the dead body in the sand.
   The police found the dead body on the sand.

3. Find the preposition:
   If you're short ... money, I can lend you some.

4. Explain the difference in meaning:
   My boss let me work overtime.
   My boss made me work overtime.

5. How do you say these words?
   a laboratory / a lavatory

6. Explain the difference in meaning:
   hire / rent

7. Which word doesn't fit, and why?
   backpack / bag / briefcase / luggage / suitcase

8. Explain the difference in meaning:
   support / tolerate

WXYZ Game Three

W Questions

1. Find the preposition:
   If you're fond ... eating pasta, let's go to an Italian restaurant tonight.

2. Explain the difference in meaning:
   Have you ever eaten a raw steak?
   Have you ever eaten a rare steak?

3. Find the preposition:
   I can't deal ... the problem and I need some help.

4. Explain the difference in meaning:
   Have you seen the desert?
   Have you seen the dessert?

5. How do you say these words?
   enough / though / rough / through

6. Explain the difference in meaning:
   ill / sick

7. Which word doesn't fit, and why?
   elderly / middle-aged / new / old / young

8. Explain the difference in meaning:
   pants / trousers

X Questions

1. Find the preposition:
   Do you belong ... a political party?

2. Explain the difference in meaning:
   These trousers don't fit me.
   These trousers don't suit me.

3. Find the preposition:
   I'm very concerned ... the damage being done to the environment.

4. Explain the difference in meaning:
   Everybody stood up when the King walked into the room.
   Everybody was standing up when the King walked into the room.

5. How do you say these words?
   desert / dessert

6. Explain the difference in meaning:
   rob / steal

7. Which word doesn't fit, and why?
   an artist / a carpenter / a musician / a potter / a sculptor

8. Explain the difference in meaning:
   an engine / a motor

Y Questions

1. Find the preposition:
   Is this class suitable ... you?

2. Explain the difference in meaning:
   When he was sawing the piece of wood, he cut his finger.
   When he was sawing the piece of wood, he cut off his finger.

3 Find the preposition:
   I hope you'll be successful ... passing your exams.

4. Explain the difference in meaning:
   Did you arrive in time for class?
   Did you arrive on time for class?

5. How do you say these words?
   massage / message

6. Explain the difference in meaning:
   envious / jealous

7. Which word doesn't fit, and why?
   a host / a hostess / a pilot / a steward / a stewardess

8. Explain the difference in meaning:
   sensible / sensitive

Z Questions

1. Find the preposition:
   You've made excellent progress and you can be proud ... yourself.

2. Explain the difference in meaning:
   They have a good cook in the kitchen.
   They have a good cooker in the kitchen.

3. Find the preposition:
   I was so involved ... the work I was doing that I completely forgot
   about the time.

4. Explain the difference in meaning:
   She passed away yesterday.
   She passed out yesterday.

5. How do you say these words?
   advice / advise

6. Explain the difference in meaning:
   an argument / a discussion

7. Which word doesn't fit, and why?
   a blouse / a bra / panties / pants / a slip

8. Explain the difference in meaning:
   embarrassed / embarrassing

WXYZ Game Four

W Questions

1. Find the preposition:
   Don't blame me ... what happened. It wasn't my fault.

2. Explain the difference in meaning:
   Everybody laughed at me.
   Everybody laughed with me.

3. Find the preposition:
   Even good teachers sometimes get impatient ... their students.

4. Explain the difference in meaning:
   He threw the ball at me.
   He threw the ball to me.

5. How do you say these words?
   suit / suite

6. Explain the difference in meaning:
   a boss / a chief

7. Which word doesn't fit, and why?
   costly / dear / expensive / priceless / worthless

8. Explain the difference in meaning:
   raise / rise

X Questions

1. Find the preposition:
   Who are you going to vote ... in the next Election?

2. Explain the difference in meaning:
   He got tired when he ran the race.
   He was tired when he ran the race.

3. Find the preposition:
   Small children are dependent ... their parents for most of their needs.

4. Explain the difference in meaning:
   I had to go to hospital yesterday.
   I had to go to the hospital yesterday.

5. How do you say these words?
   quiet / quite

6. Explain the difference in meaning:
   bring / take / fetch

7. Which word doesn't fit, and why?
   Spring / Summer / Autumn / Fall / Winter

8. Explain the difference in meaning:
   borrow / lend

Y Questions

1. Find the preposition:
   He's searching ... the perfect partner but he hasn't found her yet.

2. Explain the difference in meaning:
   He had a bath when she arrived.
   He was having a bath when she arrived.

3. Find the preposition:
   She specialises ... teaching English as a Foreign Language.

4. Explain the difference in meaning:
   I had a toothache last week.
   I've had a toothache all week.

5. How do you say these words?
   loose / lose

6. Explain the difference in meaning:
   a mistake / a fault

7. Which word doesn't fit, and why?
   a high school / a pre-school / a primary school /
   a public school / a secondary school

8. Explain the difference in meaning:
   arrive at / arrive in

Z Questions

1. Find the preposition:
   How long did it take the patient to recover ... the illness?

2. Explain the difference in meaning:
   Do you like dancing?
   Would you like to dance?

3. Find the preposition:
   It's difficult to communicate ... people when you don't speak the same language.

4. Explain the difference in meaning:
   I used to drink coffee for breakfast.
   I'm used to drinking coffee for breakfast.

5. How do you say these words?
   breath / breathe

6. Explain the difference in meaning:
   practice / practise

7. Which word doesn't fit, and why?
   biology / botany / chemistry / history / physics

8. Explain the difference in meaning:
   let / rent

Just One Chance is a game for two teams to provide controlled practice in the use of the passive. A point is awarded each time an object can be identified within thirty seconds but the clue can only be given once. There are two sets of clues, one for each team. The first player in team A reads a clue to team B and anyone in the team is allowed to answer. The process is then reversed. The two sets of clues are presented below.

Clues For Team A:

1. Once this was invented by Jacob Schick in 1928, removing your beard became a lot easier.
   Electric shaver

2. Drinks could be kept hot or cold for much longer periods of time once this was invented by James Dewar.
   Vacuum flask

3. A lot of cinemas were forced to close down due to lack of business after this was invented by Russian-born Alexander Ponatieff in 1956.
   Video recorder

4. This drink was developed in the USA in 1896 and the exact recipe has been kept a closely guarded secret ever since.
   Coca-Cola

5. Fires were put out with buckets of water until this was invented by an English army captain called George Manby 1816.
   Fire extinguisher (the first portable fire fighter)

6. Before this was invented by J. A. Wilson in 1875, the only way to open a tin of baked beans was with a hammer.
   Mechanical can opener

7. This international language was invented by a Polish man in 1887 but it has never become widely used.
   Esperanto

8. Copies of documents were made by using a piece of carbon paper in a typewriter before this was invented by Chester Carlson in 1948.
   Photocopier

9. This was first discovered in China when some leaves fell off a branch and landed in Emperor Shan Yeng's cup of hot water.
   Tea

10. Before this was invented in 1876 by Thomas Edison, you could only talk to people in other countries by travelling to them.
    Telephone

11. Once this was invented by Herbert Haddan in 1879, it became a lot easier to attach pieces of paper together.
    Stapler

12. Before this was invented by Willis Carrier in 1902, the only way to keep cool indoors was by using a fan.
    Air conditioning

Clues For Team B:

1. It became a lot more risky to drink and drive once this was invented by an American doctor called R. N. Harger in 1938.
   Breathalyser (originally called a drunkometer)

2. This was first installed in a building in 1857 and invented by Elisha Otis. If it hadn't been developed, skyscrapers would have been totally impractical.
   Lift (an "elevator" in American English)

3. Not surprisingly, this was invented by an Englishman – Arthur Large in 1922. It's often switched on when "End Of Part One" appears on the TV screen.
   Electric kettle

4. This drink was first made by a Scottish monk in 1494 and it's also produced in Ireland.
   Whisky (the Irish version is spelt "whiskey")

5. This was invented by Cornelius Drebbel in 1624 and first tried out underwater in the River Thames.
   Submarine

6. Once this was patented by Percy Spencer in 1945, cooking became a lot quicker and it can now be found in kitchens worldwide.
   Microwave

7. Although originally designed by Leonardo da Vinci, the first successful one was built by a Ukrainian called Igor Sikorsky in 1939.
   Helicopter

8. Once this was invented by a Russian called Vladimir Zworykin, the art of conversation died!
   Television (the first electronic one)

9. This musical instrument was invented by an Italian called Bartolomeo Cristofori in 1709 and its keys are made of ebony and ivory.
   Piano

10. This form of alternative medicine was first formulated by Samuel Hahnemann in 1796 and is based on the principle that like cures like.
    Homeopathy

11. Although these sweet rolls are thought to be French, they were first made in Vienna by a Polish baker.
    Croissants

12. This drink was discovered by the dervish Ali bin Omar al Shidilly when he was lost in the desert by boiling the red fruit of a plant.
    Coffee

Information Gap activities can also be used to facilitate both pair and groupwork and these can be based on articles or on pictures. Two different versions of the text/picture are prepared – A and B. Pair the A students with the B students. They then take it in turns to question each other to find the missing information.

How Weather-Sensitive Are You? (Version A)

The suggestion has been put forward that .... but can it be borne out when we look into the claim in more detail?

People all over the world simply can't cope with good weather, say biometeo-rologists, the experts who carry out research into how sunshine and showers affect our moods. London police are called on to .... , researchers in Egypt point out that the divorce rate goes up with the temperature, and riots in American cities can be put down to the long, hot summer too.

A surprising number of people find it hard to cope with .... It's important to get across the fact that feeling hot and uptight are connected because if people don't know there's a physical reason they tend to get even more worked up. British summertime can be particu-larly stressful as ....

Sunshine brings about subtle changes in our hormone balance and doctors have come up with .... This can be put down to the effect of the sun on the pineal gland, at the top of the head, which controls hormone release. Our moods, too, can be dramatically affected. Waking up irritable and snapping at everyone you meet can also be put down to the weather. On a bright sunny day when atmospheric pressure is high, people tend to .... Work output is also stepped up in such conditions.

The whole business is now taken so seriously that American TV stations put out a nightly Weather Trend index and millions tune in to find out how the weather is likely to affect them.

The weather seems to get some people down more than others. Women are generally more weather-sensitive than men, and people getting on in years tend to be more susceptible too. Excitable people are more put out by the heat than quiet, unemotional types, and geniuses turn out to be ....

According to recent research, hot and sultry weather can lead to an increase in industrial accidents. It also brings about unruly behaviour in classrooms and family members tend to ....

When the sun sizzles, it's a good idea to remove your hat. It may shade your eyes but eighty percent of body heat escapes through the top of the head so taking off your hat will help to cool you down. It's also a good idea to put on clothes made from natural fibres and to do without alcohol or spicy food. Cold drinks are also to be avoided as they make you perspire and feel even worse.

One of the advantages of this type of activity is that the role of the teacher can be kept to a minimum so as to facilitate maximum student involvement. Three examples are presented below designed for Advanced level students.

How Weather-Sensitive Are You? (Version B)

The suggestion has been put forward that sunshine does you good but can it be borne out when we look into the claim in more detail?

People all over the world simply can't cope with good weather, say biometeorologists, the experts who .... London police are called on to sort out more domestic rows during hot summers than at any other time, researchers in Egypt point out that the divorce rate goes up with the temperature, and riots in American cities can be put down to ....

A surprising number of people find it hard to cope with the situation when the sun comes out. It's important to get across .... because if people don't know there's a physical reason they tend to get even more worked up. British summertime can be particularly stressful as we're just not geared up for such conditions.

Sunshine brings about .... and doctors have come up with statistics to prove that women are more likely to conceive as a result. This can be put down to the effect of the sun on the pineal gland, at the top of the head, which controls hormone release. Our moods, too, can be dramatically affected. .... can also be put down to the weather. On a bright sunny day when atmospheric pressure is high, people tend to get along better with each other. Work output is also stepped up in such conditions.

The whole business is now taken so seriously that American TV stations put out a nightly Weather Trend index and millions tune in to ....

The weather seems to get some people down more than others. Women are generally more weather-sensitive than men, and people getting on in years tend to be more susceptible too. Excitable people are more put out by the heat than quiet, unemotional types, and geniuses turn out to be the most weather-sensitive of all.

According to recent research, hot and sultry weather can lead to .... It also brings about unruly behaviour in classrooms and family members tend to fall out with each other for no apparent reasons on such days.

When the sun sizzles, it's a good idea to remove your hat. It may shade your eyes but eighty percent of body heat escapes through the top of the head so taking off your hat will help to cool you down. It's also a good idea to put on clothes made from natural fibres and to do without .... Cold drinks are also to be avoided as they make you perspire and feel even worse.

Making Scents Of The Tube (A)

Scientists have come up with ....
....
.... A whiff of the seaside or a bracing blast of country air piped into Underground carriages would calm stressed-out commuters and help to cut down on rush-hour aggression, they claim. The smells that have turned out to be most effective are seaside salt and driftwood, reminding travellers of sun-drenched, relaxing holidays on the beach.

They put forward the claim that...
.... , cutting down brawls if pleasant smells wafted across stadiums. They would calm people down, stop them turning on each other and help to stamp out the problem of violence on the terraces.

An experiment could be carried out on the Tube to ....
.... Happy odours could be ventilated into some carriages with others left as they are. Then the difference could be looked into. Anything to calm people down on the Tube is bound to go down well with the long-suffering commuters who have to put up with the most appalling conditions, especially during the summer.

The scientists working on the project are currently making do with ....
.... but have put in for Government cash to carry on with their research. At present they are concentrating on ....
.... Someone who has to deal with extreme claustrophobia, for example, can be helped to get over it by trying out a smell that is associated with a pleasant event.

London transport have turned down ....
.... This negative attitude can probably be put down to cynicism and an aversion to change. However, the theory behind the research is based on aromatherapy, the use of essential oils, which has been around since the beginning of time. Moreover, there
is no doubt that we could all do with some help to cope with
the stress of modern day life which leads to so many
problems.

Making Scents Of The Tube (B)

Scientists have come up with a proposal which could lead to a significant breakthrough in efforts to deal with road rage and tension on public transport. A whiff of the seaside or a bracing blast of country air piped into Underground carriages would .... , they claim. The smells that have turned out to be most effective are seaside salt and driftwood, reminding travellers of sun-drenched, relaxing holidays on the beach.

They put forward the claim that the treatment would even work on football hooligans, cutting down brawls if pleasant smells wafted across stadiums. They would calm people down, stop them turning on each other and help to ....

An experiment could be carried out on the Tube to find out whether the idea worked. Happy odours could be ventilated into some carriages with others left as they are. Then the difference could be looked into. Anything to calm people down on the Tube is bound to go down well with .... , especially during the summer.

The scientists working on the project are currently making do with financial support from industry but have put in for .... At present they are concentrating on helping people who are going through severe anxiety problems. Someone who has to deal with extreme claustrophobia, for example, can be helped to get over it by trying out a smell that is associated with a pleasant event.

London transport have turned down invitations to comment on the proposals saying they want nothing to do with the project. This negative attitude can probably be put down to cynicism and an aversion to change. However, the theory behind the research is based on aromatherapy, the use of essential oils, which has been around .... Moreover, there is no doubt that we could all do with some help to cope with the stress of modern day life which leads to so many problems.

Everything You Always Wanted To Know About The Brain (A)

1. The brain is an extension of the spinal cord. It looks like a walnut kernel, is pinkish-grey and has the consistency of blancmange.

2. In the ancient world (Egypt, Mesopotamia) the brain was regarded as unimportant. Thought and emotions were attributed to ....

3. The brain is the only living part of the body that cannot feel pain.

4. The Institute of the Brain in Moscow contains Lenin's brain, slivered into 30,000 sections.

5. James I said smoking was "harmful to the brain"; studies now show that people who smoke more than a packet a day are 4.3 times more likely to develop Alzheimer's Disease than non-smokers.

6. The memory region is thought to have the potential to ....

7. The cerebrum, in the forebrain, forms a higher proportion of the human brain than in any other animal and is responsible for our unique intelligence.

8. A rough measure of intelligence is .... In humans this is about 50 to 1. In a cat it is about 4 to 1. Marmosets, at 18 to 1, rank second to humans.

9. The part of the human brain that controls the thumb is as big as an entire rat's brain.

10. Men's brains (about 1,400g) are usually heavier than women's (about 1,260g) but form a smaller percentage of body weight, at 1.9 percent to 2.1 percent. Women's brains decay evenly; men's do so more rapidly in the left hemisphere.

11. Each day a brain makes one hundred times more connections than the world's telephone system.

12. The left brain, the centre of logical thinking, controls the right hand and vice versa. .... explains why left-handedness is roughly twice as common among artists.

13. The brain consumes twenty percent of the body's oxygen supply.

14. The reputation of fish as beneficial for the brain is based on .... But exercising the brain probably does more good than any amount of marine produce.

15. Brain disorders put more people in hospital than any other affliction.

16. Brain waves actually exist - as patterns of electrical activity which can be recorded on an electroencephalograph (EEG).

17. ...., which weighed 1,565g, belonged to a murderess.

18. When the head is severed from the body, the brain can continue to function for between twenty and twenty five seconds.

Everything You Always Wanted To Know About The Brain (B)

1. The brain is an extension of the spinal cord. It looks like a walnut kernel, is pinkish-grey and has the consistency of blancmange.

2. In the ancient world (Egypt, Mesopotamia) the brain was regarded as unimportant. Thought and emotions were attributed to the stomach, liver and gall bladder.

3. The brain is the only living part of the body that cannot feel pain.

4. The Institute of the Brain in Moscow contains Lenin's brain, slivered into 30,000 sections.

5. James I said smoking was "harmful to the brain"; studies now show that people who smoke more than a packet a day are 4.3 times more likely to...........................
....

6. The memory region is thought to have the potential to receive 10 items of information every second.

7. .... forms a higher proportion of the human brain than in any other animal and is responsible for our unique intelligence.

8. A rough measure of intelligence is the ratio of the weight of the brain to that of the spinal cord. In humans this is about 50 to 1. In a cat it is about 4 to 1. Marmosets, at 18 to 1, rank second to humans.

9. The part of the human brain that controls the thumb is as big as an entire rat's brain.

10. Men's brains (about 1,400g) are usually heavier than women's (about 1,260g) but form a smaller percentage of body weight, at 1.9 per cent to 2.1 per cent. Women's brains decay evenly; men's do so more rapidly in the left hemisphere.

11. Each day a brain makes ....
....

12. The left brain, the centre of logical thinking, controls the right hand and vice versa. The fact that the right brain is stronger in visual skills explains why left-handedness is roughly twice as common among artists.

13. The brain consumes ....

14. The reputation of fish as beneficial for the brain is based on its high level of phosphorus. But exercising the brain probably does more good than any amount of marine produce.

15. Brain disorders put more people in hospital than any other affliction.

16. Brain waves actually exist – as patterns of electrical activity which can be recorded on an electroencephalograph (EEG).

17. The largest recorded female brain, which weighed 1,565g, belonged to a murderess.

18. When the head is severed from the body, the brain can continue to ....
....

Call My Bluff is an ideal way of practising defining relative clauses for an Advanced level class and the instructions for a suggested version of the game are presented below.

> Arrange yourselves into four teams. Look up the definitions of your words in a dictionary. One team member should present the true definition and three of the other team members should invent false ones. Try to make the false definitions as convincing as possible! Once the other teams have heard your definitions, they have to decide which was the correct one. If they are successful, they earn a point. However, if they are wrong the point is yours. The team with the most points wins the game.

Words For Team A:	Words For Team B:
a big-wig	a nit-wit
wishy-washy	hocus-pocus
to dilly-dally	a gee-gee
chit-chat	itsy-bitsy
a fuddy-duddy	nitty-gritty
Words For Team C:	Words For Team D:
jiggery-pokery	hanky-panky
hoity-toity	roly-poly
riff-raff	a silly-billy
mumbo-jumbo	argy-bargy
higgledy-piggledy	a pow-wow

Questionnaires also appeal to the interpersonal intelligence type as they can involve the learners working in groups together. *After pre-teaching new vocabulary, arrange the students in groups. Hand out a copy of the questionnaire to an "interviewer" in each group who reads the questions to the other students and takes on the role of the teacher. Only the interviewer should be able to see the copy and (s)he presents the questionnaire to the group as a listening activity. Meanwhile, you can circulate to provide any assistance required. The next stage is for the students to add up their scores and assess the results, which can be examined and discussed by the class as a whole. Although the material is inauthentic in that the questionnaires are contrived, the students have an authentic reason for doing the activity - to find out more about themselves.*

What Sort Of Holiday Is Right For You? (Gerunds)

1. **What kind of job do you prefer doing?**
   a. something absorbing
   b. something mechanical
   c. a desk job
   d. something that keeps you active

2. **What do you feel like doing at the end of the working day?**
   a. going straight to bed
   b. collapsing in front of the TV
   c. going out and having a good time
   d. having a hot bath or massage to help you relax

3. **How are you used to sleeping?**
   a. restlessly
   b. soundly
   c. you have difficulty in getting to sleep
   d. you keep waking up during the night

4. **What do you enjoy doing when you have a day off work?**
   a. going for a drive in a fast car
   b. being away from the office
   c. catching up on the housework
   d. doing absolutely nothing

5. **What kind of film are you keen on?**
   a. an action-packed adventure
   b. one with a complicated plot
   c. something true to life
   d. an escapist fantasy

6. **How would you feel about having to retire tomorrow?**
   a. take it in your stride
   b. not know what to do with yourself
   c. miss your colleagues
   d. look forward to it

7. **What sort of clothes are you fond of wearing?**
   a. elegant
   b. fashionable
   c. hardwearing
   d. clothes you feel comfortable in

8. **What type of food are you into eating?**
   a. a large steak
   b. anything as long as someone else cooks it
   c. fish and chips
   d. something exotic

Check Your Score

1. a-2 b-1 c-0 d-3
2. a-1 b-0 c-2 d-3
3. a-0 b-1 c-3 d-2
4. a-1 b-2 c-3 d-0
5. a-3 b-2 c-0 d-1
6. a-1 b-2 c-0 d-3
7. a-2 b-3 c-1 d-0
8. a-3 b-1 c-0 d-2

What Your Score Means

0-6   You're probably not used to doing much exercise at work so an active holiday would be good for you. But be careful you don't overdo things.

7-12   You're the kind of person who enjoys being on the go so a touring holiday would probably appeal to you. Make sure you plan it realistically.

13-18 You seem to be a bit of a workaholic so you would benefit from choosing a holiday to take your mind off things - maybe an "activity" holiday, like skiing, sailing or golf.

19-24 You're probably the kind of person who has difficulty in letting your hair down so choose something that keeps you occupied most of the time in a resort which has plenty of nightlife.

How Secure Do You Feel In Your Job? (make/do)

1. How often do you make everyone aware of the long hours you do at work?
   a. frequently   b. sometimes   c. rarely   d. never

2. How regularly do you make an earlier start than your colleagues?
   a. frequently   b. sometimes   c. rarely   d. never

3. How often do you make the effort to go to work even when you could do with time off sick?
   a. frequently   b. sometimes   c. rarely   d. never

4. Do you ever make do with shorter holiday breaks than you're entitled to?
   a. frequently   b. sometimes   c. rarely   d. never

5. Are you ever tempted to leave your computer on to make it appear that you worked late?
   a. frequently   b. sometimes   c. rarely   d. never

6. Have you ever made it clear to your boss that you're available night and day if required?
   a. frequently   b. sometimes   c. rarely   d. never

7. Do you make a point of letting your boss know about your successes?
   a. frequently   b. sometimes   c. rarely   d. never

8. Do you ever feel the need to make your presence felt at a meeting by some "clever" or attention-seeking comment?
   a. frequently   b. sometimes   c. rarely   d. never

9. Do you do your best to appear to be busy whenever your boss makes an appearance?
   a. frequently   b. sometimes   c. rarely   d. never

10. How often do you do unnecessary overtime just to make a good impression?
    a. frequently   b. sometimes   c. rarely   d. never

Check Your Score

1. a-3 b-2 c-1 d-0
2. a-3 b-2 c-1 d-0
3. a-3 b-2 c-1 d-0
4. a-3 b-2 c-1 d-0
5. a-3 b-2 c-1 d-0
6. a-3 b-2 c-1 d-0
7. a-3 b-2 c-1 d-0
8. a-3 b-2 c-1 d-0
9. a-3 b-2 c-1 d-0
10. a-3 b-2 c-1 d-0

What Your Score Means

0-10   It's clear you've got nothing to worry about. You feel secure in your job and show few signs of suffering from presenteeism – self-imposed chaining to the desk.

11-20 Although you feel somewhat insecure, it's fortunately not overwhelming. Your behaviour at work only marginally affects your personal life.

21-30 Your need to create a good impression suggests you're unfortunately far from feeling secure. Ask yourself how much this is due to your own sense of inadequacy rather than the nature of your position at work.

How Many Friends Do You Have?

1. **What do your colleagues do when you get to work in the morning?**
   a. smile and ask you how you are
   b. nod brief acknowledgement
   c. ignore you

2. **If you wanted to, could you spend every night of the week socialising with different people?**
   a. yes
   b. no
   c. only occasionally

3. **What happened the last time you went to a party?**
   a. it was one of several you were invited to that night
   b. you didn't know the host and you went as somebody's guest
   c. it was the first you had been invited to for ages

4. **How often do you have to turn down an invitation because of a prior engagement?**
   a. sometimes
   b. often
   c. never

5. **How many birthday cards did you get last year?**
   a. more than 20
   b. 10-19
   c. 5-9
   d. 0-4

6. **Who are you most likely to receive a Valentine's Day card from?**
   a. a secret admirer
   b. your partner
   c. your mother

7. **Do you ever find yourself at a party with nobody to talk to?**
   a. never
   b. sometimes
   c. usually

8. **How often do you unplug your phone or switch on the answering machine because you want to avoid calls?**
   a. often
   b. never
   c. sometimes

9. **Are your social activities usually the result of your own actions or the result of other people's?**
   a. the result of your own actions
   b. other people usually contact you
   c. a mixture of both

10. **When did you last receive an unexpected visit from a friend?**
    a. last week
    b. last month
    c. more than a month ago

Check Your Score

1. a-2 b-1 c-0
2. a-3 b-0 c-1
3. a-3 b-0 c-1
4. a-1 b-2 c-0
5. a-3 b-2 c-1 d-0
6. a-2 b-1 c-0
7. a-2 b-1 c-0
8. a-2 b-0 c-1
9. a-0 b-2 c-1
10. a-2 b-1 c-0

What Your Score Means

1-8   If you want to be more popular, try being nicer to people. You'll find that, in general, you get what you give.

9-16   Although you're averagely popular, other people don't like you as much as you might wish. Try building up your self-confidence.

17-23   You're a social butterfly and probably consider yourself to be extremely popular. But how many of your friends are good ones?

How Well-Balanced Are You?

1. **Do you find that you can trust people?**
   a. absolutely everybody
   b. most people
   c. a few people
   d. nobody

2. **How often do you worry about your health?**
   a. often
   b. sometimes
   c. never

3. **Would being in debt worry you?**
   a. not at all
   b. a little
   c. a lot

4. **How often do you wash your hands before you eat?**
   a. always
   b. sometimes
   c. never

5. **If you saw a child or animal suffer, would it upset you?**
   a. yes
   b. no

6. **How often does your mood go up and down?**
   a. almost hourly
   b. several times a day
   c. every few days
   d. hardly ever

7. **If you were found crying, would you allow someone to comfort you?**
   a. never
   b. only a close friend
   c. yes

8. **How often do you worry about things you should have done or said?**
   a. all the time
   b. often
   c. sometimes
   d. never

9. **If someone else found your partner attractive, would you get upset?**
   a. it would depend on who it was
   b. not usually
   c. often

10. **Would you be embarrassed if a member of your family walked around the house naked?**
    a. extremely
    b. a little
    c. not at all

11. **Does it worry you when you make mistakes at work?**
    a. never
    b. only if they're big ones
    c. all the time

12. **How concerned are you about your appearance?**
    a. very
    b. a little
    c. not at all

Check Your Score

1.   a-0   b-2   c-1   d-0
2.   a-0   b-2   c-1
3.   a-0   b-2   c-1
4.   a-0   b-2   c-1
5.   a-2   b-0
6.   a-0   b-0   c-1   d-2
7.   a-0   b-1   c-2
8.   a-0   b-0   c-2   d-1
9.   a-1   b-2   c-0
10.   a-0   b-1   c-2
11.   a-0   b-2   c-1
12.   a-0   b-2   c-1

What Your Score Means

0-6   You're definitely a worrier and you can also be rather callous at times. Some people would say you're immature.

7-12   Although you have your share of worries, you usually manage to cope with life. However, you could manage even better. Don't forget you have the power to do something about your problems and you don't have to be a victim of circumstance.

13-18   You're mentally stable and socially mature with little to worry about. You're very unlikely to suffer from phobias or depression – but you probably knew that anyway.

19-24   You're extremely well-balanced and sane – a highly optimistic and resilient individual, with no need to do this test.

How Creative Are You?

1. **How do you behave when you have young children to look after?**
    a. play games with them and try to make them laugh
    b. make sure they are disciplined and properly behaved
    c. keep them clean and away from danger

2. **Which of the following would you buy as a second home?**
    a. an old mansion house with character
    b. a bungalow on a housing estate
    c. a time-share apartment

3. **If you could adopt an animal in the zoo and visit it regularly, which one would you choose?**
    a. a panther
    b. a guinea pig
    c. an elephant

4. **What kind of people do you like to have as friends?**
    a. fun-loving, unpredictable people
    b. honest and reliable types
    c. wealthy, well-known people

5. **If you were having friends for dinner, what would you prepare?**
    a. experiment with an unusual and exotic dish
    b. serve a roast and two vegetables
    c. stick to a tried and tested recipe

6. **What attitude do you take when you have a boring and repetitive task to do?**
    a. try to recall amusing incidents to keep you awake
    b. accept that certain things have to be done whether you like it or not
    c. get the job over with as soon as possible

7. **How would you choose to lose weight?**
    a. by turning raw fruit and vegetables into a visual feast
    b. by cutting out starch and sugar
    c. by counting your calories

8. **What do you do when you can't get to sleep?**
    a. close your eyes and drift into a world of fantasy
    b. try counting sheep
    c. take a sleeping pill

9. **What sort of books do you like reading?**
    a. adventure stories packed with action and scandal
    b. autobiographies
    c. romantic love stories

10. **Which type of TV programme would you prefer to watch?**
    a. a cartoon or a comedy
    b. a family quiz show
    c. an American "cop" movie

What Your Score Means

If you've scored mostly "a"s, you're probably a creative and imaginative person. You're an unconventional person and you like to be different, which sometimes gets you into trouble. If you want to be more accepted by others, try to adopt a more conventional attitude to life.

If you've scored mostly "b"s, you're likely to be an orderly and respectable person, but a bit too concerned about doing the right thing at the right time. Try not to bottle up your feelings as this could lead to tension. It would do you good to let your hair down once in a while.

If you've scored mostly "c"s, you're basically a rather conventional type who follows the crowd. Allow yourself freedom to express your originality instead of being a slave to fashion and stop worrying about what others think of you all the time.

Are You A Workaholic?

1. How often do you get up early in the morning?
   a. always
   b. sometimes
   c. never

2. How often are you the first person to arrive at the office?
   a. always
   b. sometimes
   c. never

3. When you're on holiday, do you find it difficult to relax and stop thinking about work?
   a. often
   b. sometimes
   c. never

4. How often do you make daily lists of "things to do"?
   a. always
   b. sometimes
   c. never

5. Do you find it hard to "do nothing" for any length of time?
   a. definitely
   b. never
   c. it depends on the situation

6. Do you read or work while you're eating?
   a. often
   b. sometimes
   c. never

7. Have you ever been advised to slow down and take things easy?
   a. yes
   b. no

8. How often do you take work home with you in the evenings?
   a. often
   b. sometimes
   c. never

9. Are you reluctant to delegate tasks at work?
   a. yes
   b. no

10. How often do you work over the weekend?
   a. usually
   b. sometimes
   c. never

Check Your Score

1.   a-2   b-1   c-0
2.   a-2   b-1   c-0
3.   a-2   b-1   c-0
4.   a-2   b-1   c-0
5.   a-2   b-0   c-1
6.   a-2   b-1   c-0
7.   a-2   b-0
8.   a-2   b-1   c-0
9.   a-2   b-0
10.   a-2   b-1   c-0

What Your Score Means

0-5   You seem to be positively workaphobic!

6-10   You know how to maintain a reasonable balance between work and fun.

11-15   You work so hard that you run the risk of damaging your health.

16-20   Are you using work to escape from problems in other areas of your life? Have you got your priorities right?

And to conclude this chapter, here are two examples of role-plays you might like to try out on your classes.

The Fur Trade

The Setting
You're going to take part in a discussion on the radio or the TV. The subject is the fur trade. In addition to the presenter, three other people are involved – a spokesperson for LYNX (fighting the fur trade), a Government Minister under pressure to introduce new legislation, and a well-known actress who regularly wears fur coats.

The Format
Work in groups of four. Choose your roles and make notes on the points you'd like to make. The presenter's role is to introduce the programme and the speakers, to ensure that everyone has the opportunity to put across their views, and then to draw the discussion to a close. When you feel ready, you can record the programme on cassette and/or act it out in front of the rest of the class.

The Aliens

The Setting
You're being interviewed by a reporter from a national newspaper about a strange encounter you had. You were transported by a group of aliens to another planet but somehow you managed to survive and returned to tell your story.

The Format
Work in pairs. The reporter should prepare some questions to find out when and where the incident took place, what the aliens looked like, why they took the interviewee with them, and how he or she managed to return. The interviewee should prepare a plausible account of what took place. When you feel ready, you can record the interview on cassette and/or act it out in front of the rest of the group. As a follow-up activity, you could write an account of your adventure or a newspaper article based on the interview.

Unit 5: How To Cater For Logical-Mathematical Intelligence

Students who enjoy science subjects and working with computers are likely to have a high degree of logical-mathematical intelligence. These people are problem-solvers, capable of both deductive and inductive reasoning. They appreciate precision and like organising information by sequencing and prioritising it.

The OHE Model presented by Michael Lewis in *The Lexical Approach* – observe, hypothesis and experiment – is ideally suited to catering for logical-mathematical intelligence. The activity presented below is designed for Elementary students to elicit and provide practice in the use of the articles. It takes the form of a picture composition.

Take a piece of paper and draw a square on it. Put a triangle on top to make a roof and then add a chimney with smoke coming out. Now draw a rectangle to make a front door for your house, two squares to make windows downstairs and two squares for windows upstairs. Add a tree on each side of the house to make a garden, a man holding a flower with a smile on his face and a large cat sitting next to him. Finally draw a circle to make a sun and a couple of clouds.

Colour the leaves on the trees green and the trunks of the trees brown. Colour the flower the man is holding red and the cat black. Colour the sun yellow and the clouds grey or white.

Why is the indefinite article used to describe the shapes and figures to be drawn and the definite article to describe the colours?

Work in pairs and take it in turns to give your partner a picture to draw and to colour. Use the example above as a model.

Crosswords are popular with problem-solvers and the *Phrasal Verb Grids* presented below will enable learners to make use of their talents in this field. The grids are topic-based as categorising the phrasal verbs in this way can make them easier to learn. This also makes it easier to relate the activities to the topics that appear in the course book being used. The aim is for the learners to match the numbers with the letters to find the phrasal verbs with the meanings given in the grid. In each case, either a number or a letter is given to provide an additional clue. Once these answers have been checked, the students are then given the opportunity to use them in context by fitting them into the gaps in the sentences.

Politics

Match the numbers with the letters to find the phrasal verbs with the meanings given in the grids.

1 step		2 pull		3 stand
	4 bring		5 call	
6 turn		7 cross		8 rule
	9 put		10 get	
A on		B across		C off
	D down		E up	
F for		G over		H out
	I back		J through	

to resign	3	
to convey		B
to delay	9	
to increase (in intensity)		E
to survive	2	
to discount		H
to restore	4	
to attack		A
to defect	7	
to demand		F

Answers

3 - D
10 - B
9 - C
1 - E
2 - J
8 - H
4 - I
6 - A
7 - G
5 - F

Now use each of the phrasal verbs once only to complete the following sentences:

1. There has been a lot of pressure on the Prime Minister to ... in favour of someone younger.

2. Do you think the Prime Minister will manage to ... despite all the recent difficulties? Personally, I strongly doubt it.

3. When the former Cabinet Minister ... to the other side, she was shunned by all her old colleagues.

4. The Prime Minister will probably ... calling a General Election until the last possible minute in the hope that the Government's popularity might have improved by then.

5. If there is no decisive majority, the possibility of a second Election cannot be ... .

6. The problem with this Government is their failure to ... their message ... to the voters.

7. The Leader of the Opposition ... the disloyal members of the Shadow Cabinet by demoting them in a reshuffle.

8. The resignation of the Minister of Transport was ... once his involvement in the scandal became known.

9. There in no point in ... capital punishment as there is no evidence to suggest it would act as a deterrent to would-be criminals.

10. The Opposition campaign against the Government is being ... in an attempt to force an early Election.

Answers

1. stand down
2. pull through
3. crossed over
4. put off
5. ruled out
6. get across
7. turned on
8. called for
9. bringing back
10. stepped up

Health & Medicine

Match the numbers with the letters to find the phrasal verbs with the meanings given in the grids.

1 get		2 pull		3 come
	4 pull		5 do	
6 put		7 carry		8 pass
	9 cut		10 give	
A to		B over		C on
	D out		E through	
F up		G away		H down
	I with		J off	

to continue	7	
to recover from		B
to stop	10	
to benefit from		I
to die	8	
to regain consciousness		A
to extract	2	
to reduce		H
to delay	6	
to survive		E

Answers

7 - C
1 - B
10 - F
5 - I
8 - G
3 - A
4 - D
9 - H
6 - J
2 - E

Now use each of the phrasal verbs once only to complete the following sentences:

1. It took the patient a long time to ... the operation.

2. When she ... , she'd like to be cremated.

3. If you ... working so hard, you'll end up by having a breakdown.

4. You're clearly exhausted and could ... a break from work.

5. I ... making an appointment for as long as possible in the hope that the problem would just go away without any need for treatment.

6. Unless you ... smoking, you can seriously damage your health.

7. If you find it difficult to stop completely, at least try to ... the number you smoke each day.

8. The patient is on the critical list and it's unlikely that he'll ... .

9. I'm afraid two of your wisdom teeth will have to be ... because they've become infected.

10. When I ... after the accident, I found myself lying in a hospital bed.

Answers

1. get over
2. passes away
3. carry on
4. do with
5. put off
6. give up
7. cut down
8. pull through
9. taken out
10. came to

Crime & Punishment

Match the numbers with the letters to find the phrasal verbs with the meanings given in the grids.

1 break		2 turn		3 bring
	4 call		5 come	
6 keep		7 own		8 rule
	9 give		10 make	
A off		B for		C on
	D up to		E into	
F back		G by		H back
	I down		J out	

to enter (using force)	1	
to return		H
to find	5	
to continue		C
to escape	10	
to restore		F
to admit	7	
to demand		B
to refuse	2	
to discount		J

Answers

1 - E
9 - H
5 - G
6 - C
10 - A
3 - F
7 - D
4 - B
2 - I
8 - J

Now use each of the phrasal verbs once only to complete the following sentences:

1. If you ... breaking the law, it's only a matter of time before you get caught.

2. The lawyer applied for bail on behalf of his client but was ... by the judge.

3. If you ... having committed the crime, you'll make life a lot easier for yourself.

4. The robbers ... in a getaway car that was parked outside the bank.

5. Unless you ... the money you stole, I'll have no choice but to inform the police.

6. The police wanted to know how the suspect had managed to ... such a large sum of money.

7. If the demonstrators gets out of hand, the use of force cannot be ... .

8. Do you really believe that ... capital punishment would help to reduce the crime rate? Personally, I strongly doubt it.

9. The burglars ... the house while the owner was away on holiday.

10. Some right wing members of the Government are ... tougher sentencing by judges.

Answers

1. keep on
2. turned down
3. own up to
4. made off
5. give back
6. come by
7. ruled out
8. bringing back
9. broke into
10. calling for

The World Of Work

Match the numbers with the letters to find the phrasal verbs with the meanings given in the grids.

1 lay		2 get		3 look
	4 go		5 break	
6 take		7 pull		8 turn
	9 set		10 stand	
A aside		B over		C into
	D down		E up	
F off		G up for		H by
	I through		J on	

to examine	3	
to check		B
to arrive	8	
to survive		I
to employ	6	
to make redundant		F
to defend	10	
to manage		H
to fail	5	
to resolve		A

Answers

3 - C
4 - B
8 - E
7 - I
6 - J
1 - F
10 - G
2 - H
5 - D
9 - A

Now use each of the phrasal verbs once only to complete the following sentences:

1. We need to ... ways of reducing costs or we're unlikely to survive the current financial crisis.

2. During the height of the season most hotels ... extra staff.

3. If you ... late for work again, you'll get into serious trouble.

4. Don't let your boss take advantage of you – ... your rights.

5. Unfortunately the talks between the management and the union ... as they were unable to reach an agreement.

6. Unless they can ... their differences, they're not going to get very far.

7. I can't ... on my salary and I'm finding it difficult to make ends meet.

8. As there was a fall in demand for the product, a number of workers in the factory had to be ... .

9. Unless we can improve our sales figures, we're unlikely to ... .

10. You'd better ... the figures again to make sure you haven't made a mistake.

Answers

1. look into
2. take on
3. turn up
4. stand up for
5. broke down
6. set aside
7. get by
8. laid off
9. pull through
10. go over

Relationships

Match the numbers with the letters to find the phrasal verbs with the meanings given in the grids.

1 look		2 do		3 stand
	4 go		5 get	
6 take		7 split		8 feel
	9 break		10 turn	
A up		B for		C down
	D off		E to	
F on		G over		H out with
	I by		J with	

to reject	10	
to sympathise with		B
to part	7	
to develop a liking for		F
to end	9	
to recover from		G
to support	3	
to benefit from		J
to regard	1	
to have a relationship with		H

Answers

10 - C
8 - B
7 - A
6 - E
9 - D
5 - G
3 - I
2 - J
1 - F
4 - H

Now use each of the phrasal verbs once only to complete the following sentences:

1. I asked my girlfriend to marry me but she ... me ... .

2. They ... their relationship because they decided that they were basically incompatible.

3. Although they ... , they remained good friends.

4. When you left me for my best friend, it broke my heart and I don't think I'll ever ... it.

5. I ... you as one of my very closest friends.

6. Our relationship has been under a great deal of strain recently and I feel we could both ... a break.

7. I promise I'll ... you through thick and thin – you can depend on me.

8. How long have they been ... each other?

9. I know what you must be going through and I ... you.

10. I ... you from the very first moment we met.

Answers

1. turned down
2. broke off
3. split up
4. get over
5. look on
6. do with
7. stand by
8. going out with
9. feel for
10. took to

Food & Drink

Match the numbers with the letters to find the phrasal verbs with the meanings given in the grids.

1 come		2 throw		3 clear
	4 put		5 run	
6 go		7 turn		8 get
	9 cut		10 do	
A off		B through		C on
	D out of		E away	
F with		G down		H out
	I up		J by	

to remove	3	
to prove to be		H
to reduce	9	
to benefit from		F
to find	1	
to add		C
to vomit	2	
to be bad		A
to finish	8	
to have none left		D

Answers

3 - E
7 - H
9 - G
10 - F
1 - J
4 - C
2 - I
6 - A
8 - B
5 - D

Now use each of the phrasal verbs once only to complete the following sentences:

1. How on earth do you expect me to ... all this? You've given me enough food to feed an army!

2. Now that you've all finished eating, I'll ... the plates.

3. The food tasted disgusting and made me want to ... .

4. I'm starving and I could ... something to eat.

5. How did you manage to ... such delicious fresh strawberries at this time of the year?

6. The only way to lose weight is by ... on your daily intake of calories.

7. The meal ... to be a lot better than I'd expected.

8. The milk tastes a bit funny – I think it's ... .

9. I'm afraid we've ... coffee – will tea do?

10. The reason why you keep ... weight is that you eat too many sweets and chocolates.

Answers

1. get through
2. clear away
3. throw up
4. do with
5. come by
6. cutting down
7. turned out
8. gone off
9. run out of
10. putting on

Travelling

Match the numbers with the letters to find the phrasal verbs with the meanings given in the grids.

1 put		2 call		3 run
	4 speed		5 slow	
6 set		7 make		8 get
	9 go		10 check	
A down		B away		C up
	D on		E in	
F for		G out of		H by
	I out		J off	

to start (a journey)	6	
to pass		H
to reduce speed	5	
to extinguish		I
to increase speed	4	
to visit		D
to go in the direction of	7	
to escape		B
to have none left	3	
to register		E

Answers

6 - J
9 - H
5 - A
1 - I
4 - C
2 - D
7 - F
8 - B
3 - G
10 - E

Now use each of the phrasal verbs once only to complete the following sentences:

1. I hope we don't ... petrol or we'll be in a real mess.

2. Unless you ... , we're going to be late.

3. We ... early to avoid getting caught in the rush-hour traffic.

4. ... your cigarettes and fasten your seatbelts because the plane is about to land.

5. Unless you ... , you're in danger of having an accident.

6. This is like a magical mystery tour because I've got no idea where we're ... !

7. I'd like to ... from London for a few days by the sea.

8. The next time you're in London, I hope you'll ... me.

9. I'll meet you in the hotel lobby after you've ... .

10. As time ... , travelling from one country to another will become a lot easier.

Answers

1. run out of
2. speed up
3. set off
4. put out
5. slow down
6. making for
7. get away
8. call on
9. checked in
10. goes by

Education

Match the numbers with the letters to find the phrasal verbs with the meanings given in the grids.

1 take		2 put		3 catch
	4 hand		5 turn	
6 brush		7 carry		8 keep
	9 go		10 get	
A up with		B in		C across
	D at		E on	
F out		G over		H up on
	I round		J through	

to improve	6	
to repeat		G
to distribute	4	
to reach the same level as		A
to absorb	1	
to pass		J
to express	2	
to persevere with		D
to continue	7	
to prove to be		F

Answers

6 - H
9 - G
4 - I
3 - A
1 - B
10 - J
2 - C
8 - D
7 - E
5 - F

Now use each of the phrasal verbs once only to complete the following sentences:

1. It's difficult to ... studying when you give me so little encouragement.

2. Although he's clearly an expert in his field, he's not very good at ... his ideas ...

3. If you're prepared to ... it, I'm sure you'll master the subject in the end.

4. I'll ... the instructions again to make sure you understand what to do.

5. Do you think she'll manage to ... the exam?

6. I thought the course was going to be interesting but it ... to be a complete waste of time.

7. Although you've missed a lot of classes, if you work hard you should be able to ... the others.

8. I can't ... any more new information – I need a break.

9. The teacher asked one of the students to ... the dictionaries.

10. I went to a language school when I arrived in London to ... my English.

Answers

1. carry on
2. putting across
3. keep at
4. go over
5. get through
6. turned out
7. catch up with
8. take in
9. hand round
10. brush up on

Guided discovery activities can also be employed to elicit spelling rules instead of providing them and an example of this is presented below on the following page.

The -ing Ending

Use the examples to work out the rules:

adding	budgeting	coping	digging
dyeing	dying	expecting	falling
fastening	feeling	forbidding	forgetting
lunging	marrying	marvelling	meeting
offering	propelling	reading	robbing
sitting	swinging	wrecking	worrying

- The infinitive remains unchanged when ... .

- The final consonant of the infinitive is doubled when ... .

- In two-syllable words the doubling only occurs when ... .

- When the infinitive ends in -e, ...

- The exceptions to these rules are ... .

Answers

- The infinitive remains unchanged when it ends with two consonants or two vowels followed by a final consonant.

- The final consonant of the infinitive is doubled when it ends with one vowel followed by one consonant.

- In two-syllable words the doubling only occurs when the stress falls on the second syllable.

- When the infinitive ends in -e, the -e is dropped.

- The exceptions to these rules are two syllable words that end in -l and when confusion could be caused – die dying/dye dying, for example.

Ordering activities involve the use of logic and two samples designed to practise phrasal verbs and idioms are presented below. In both cases, the material is topic-based – the former deals with the world of work and the latter with relationships. However, the "attack" is two-pronged as the idioms are also grouped according to verbs – in the first case the verb is *put,* and in the second activity the verb is *take.*

Read through the following extracts, then rearrange them in the correct order to make a story:

a. All the suggestions I've put forward to build up the business have been ignored and he's put a damper on all my enthusiasm.

b. Fortunately I've managed to put by enough over the years to live on until I find what I'm looking for, and my brother has offered to put me up free of charge so I can save on rent.

c. I'm sick and tired of constantly being put down by my boss and I can't put up with the situation any longer.

d. I can only put it down to the fact that I'm considerably older than him and the age difference makes him feel insecure.

e. I even put in for a transfer to another branch of the company but unfortunately to no avail.

f. I feel extremely put out by the way I've been treated, especially since the output of the factory has doubled in the time that I've been there.

g. I've been thinking about leaving for some time now but I've put off making a move in the hope that the situation might improve.

h. I wish I'd never accepted the job in the first place but I can't put the clock back. All I can do for now is put on a brave face and do my best to maintain my self-respect.

i. The lack of confidence my boss shows in me is extremely off-putting and I'm hard put to it to explain his attitude.

Answers

1-c
2-g
3-e
4-i
5-d
6-a
7-b
8-f
9-h

Read through the passage, then fill in the gaps with the correct sentences:

Taken For A Ride

I **took to** Miranda the first time we met because she was the sort of person who knows how to **take me out of myself.** She was also extremely **quick on the uptake.** She was a student who worked part-time in a Chinese **takeaway** restaurant. **1.** ... One of the things I remember about the evening was how stunning Miranda looked when she **took off** her coat. **2.** ... I think one of the reasons why I was so drawn to her was the fact that she **took after** my mother. Even now after all this time it's difficult to **take in** what she did because the experience really **took me apart.** After we'd been going out together for several months, I discovered that she'd **taken up with** my best friend and was two-timing me. **3.** ... I **took back** the engagement ring I'd given her and told her I never wanted to see her again. **4.** ... My assistant **took it on himself** to tell me how they felt and suggested that I should **take up** Karate as an outlet for my pent-up emotions. **5.** ... However, perhaps I'm being a bit unfair to her because **it takes two to make a quarrel** and I'm far from perfect myself. Anyway, hopefully I've learnt from the experience and in future I'll be less gullible.

a. As you can imagine, I was completely **taken aback** when I found out that I'd been **taken in.**

b. I felt really angry for a long time afterwards and **took it out on** my colleagues at work, who got really fed up with me.

c. I'd clearly **taken on** more than I could handle with Miranda and she'd **taken me for a ride.**

d. I **took her out** on a blind date, which was organised by a mutual friend.

e. She also made me laugh a lot by **taking off** various celebrities.

Answers

1-d
2-e
3-a
4-b
5-c

Two further examples of ordering activities are presented below. The first is a two-part dialogue on the subject of cooking to practise conditionals, and the second deals with the word order employed when inverting conditional sentences.

This is a dialogue between two friends, Peter and David, on the subject of cooking. Place the parts of the dialogue in the correct order:

a. Peter: Can't we start with something a bit more basic – what about how to boil an egg?

b. Peter: Don't be silly – I'm just pulling your leg!

c. David: If you don't know that by now, then there's really no hope for you!

d. Peter: If you got married one day, would you expect your wife to do all the cooking or would you be prepared to lend a hand?

e. Peter: I suppose I just can't be bothered. If I'd studied cookery at school when I was younger, things might have been very different. But you can't teach an old dog new tricks.

f. David: It certainly isn't! It's high time you changed your ways! In fact, I think you should start right now – I'm going to teach you how to make an omelette!

g. David: It depends. If she didn't have a full-time job, I would. But if we both worked, then I suppose we'd share it. The same applies to the housework. What about you?

h. Peter: That's certainly true – I'd save myself a fortune if I learnt how to cook. Most evenings I get myself a takeaway – fish and chips or a pizza – otherwise I just open a tin. It's not a very healthy diet.

i. David: That's rubbish! I can quote proverbs too – it's never too late to learn! And think of all the money you'd save!

j. David: Then why don't you take the trouble to learn?

k. Peter: Well, in theory I'd like the same sort of set-up. But I'm at a dead loss when it comes to cooking, so it wouldn't work out very well.

1. ....
2. ....
3. ....
4. ....
5. ....
6. ....
7. ....
8. ....
9. ....
10. ....
11. ....

In written English, for emphasis, certain conditional forms can be inverted. Look at these examples:

If anyone should phone while I'm out, ask them to leave a message.
Should anyone phone while I'm out, ask them to leave a message.

If the Government were to lose the Election, it would be a disaster.
Were the Government to lose the Election, it would be a disaster.

If I'd known you were going to phone, I'd have stayed at home.
Had I known you were going to phone, I'd have stayed at home.

Notice that SHOULD + PLAIN INFINITIVE in the IF clause is used to show that an event is unlikely. WERE TO + INFINITIVE fulfils the same function in the IF clause of a second conditional. As these are written forms, contractions cannot be used in the opening clauses.

Put the words in the following sentences in the correct order to produce inversions like the examples above:

1. any call don't help hesitate me need should to you

2. be for high it not recession so the unemployment were wouldn't

3. carefully do you have had instructions read the to understand what you you'd

4. a believe difficult find flying it saucer see to to were you you'd

5. a else had have I'd made me something told vegetarian were you you

6. anything crop find know me should to up where you

7. ago been encouragement for given had have I'd it long not up your

8. a a bath body dead find having in nightmare the think to were were you you you'd

9. address any at be contact following if me problems should the there

10. any been been called had have police the there trouble wouldn't

Exposing students to errors at lower levels can be counter-productive as it can re-inforce the errors you are attempting to eradicate. However, activities like the examples presented below can be effective with higher level students for revision purposes. Asking the learners to find the deliberate mistakes requires both the ability on their part to be analytical and also the use of logic. Each worksheet is topic-based and the sentences contain one, two or three deliberate mistakes. The students are required to circle the number of mistakes they can find, then compare their answers with those of their partner to see whether they agree with each other. As an added incentive, they could even "bet" on the outcome and they could be issued with a certain number of points or tokens to use for the purpose.

How Many Mistakes? Each sentence contains one, two or three deliberate mistakes. Circle the number of mistakes you can find, then compare your answers with those of your partner to see whether you agree with each other:

1. I prefer living in country than living in the city because there is less polluted there.   1 / 2 / 3

2. I'm looking forward to have a place of my own one day. It's something I've always dreamed of.   1 / 2 / 3

3. You'll only be eligible to a mortgage if you can show you're in a regular full-time employment.   1 / 2 / 3

4. Instead of to pay a decorator to paint your flat, it would have been a lot cheaper to do a job yourself.   1 / 2 / 3

5. In addition to be more peaceful, a countryside is also less polluted.   1 / 2 / 3

6. A fact of the matter is that I've got used to live in big cities as I was born and brought up in one.   1 / 2 / 3

7. A tenant is a person who lets a room, a flat or a house from a landlord.   1 / 2 / 3

8. The main feature of the flat is the kitchen as it comes fully equipped with all the latest labour-saving apparatus – a microwave, a washing machine, a cooker and a dishwasher.   1 / 2 / 3

9. It's high time that the government should have introduced measures to help the homeless. The current state of affairs is an absolute disgrace.   1 / 2 / 3

10. I don't know what you're complaining about because you're lucky to have a roof on your head and your situation could be a lot worse.   1 / 2 / 3

11. An accommodation on the outskirts of London is much cheaper than in the centre.   1 / 2 / 3

12. How long time did you say have you been living here? I was under an impression that you'd only just moved in but I was clearly mistaken.   1 / 2 / 3

How Many Mistakes? Each sentence contains one, two or three deliberate mistakes. Circle the number of mistakes you can find, then compare your answers with those of your partner to see whether you agree with each other:

1. Do professional footballers merit all the money they earn or do you consider them as grossly overpaid?   1 / 2 / 3

2. Certain sports can turn out to be quite expensive to take up because you need to buy lots of equipments.   1 / 2 / 3

3. I wasn't disappointed to see the Champion lose because it's good to see the underdog do well as a change.   1 / 2 / 3

4. There's no doubt at all on mind that sports in schools should be made compulsory as a healthy body makes a healthy mind.   1 / 2 / 3

5. The Captain of the team had to limp off the pitch after only ten minutes of the play so they had to bring in a substitute. 1 / 2 / 3

6. Boxing is a barbaric sport that can result in permanent brain damages or even the death and it's high time the authorities should have banned it.   1 / 2 / 3

7. Despite of having one of their players sent off and being down to ten men, they still managed to win the match.   1 / 2 / 3

8. If will smoke like a chimney and drink like a fish, you can't expect to keep yourself fit. A problem with you is that you're your own worst enemy!   1 / 2 / 3

9. The only way to improve health of the nation is by spending money on providing more amenities for sports.   1 / 2 / 3

10. It's become quite fashionable these days to join a Health Club, not only to keep fit but too as a way of making new friends.   1 / 2 / 3

11. Health Farms cater for people who want to loose their weight or change their lifestyles but can only be afforded by the wealthy. A man in the street has to find other alternatives.   1 / 2 / 3

12. One way of reducing the stress is by taking up meditation or another forms of relaxation. Alternatively, you might like to consider something more active – jogging, for example.   1 / 2 / 3

Examining pairs of words that are often confused and/or misused can provide learners with an opportunity to use their problem-solving talents. Four topic-based passages are presented below designed for this purpose.

Choose the correct answer from each pair of alternatives. (Sometimes both words are acceptable.)

I've tried **1. losing/to lose** weight **2. by/through** cutting **3. back/down** on fattening things **4. like/such as** sweets and chocolates. **5. However/Moreover,** to **6. say/tell** you the truth, all my efforts **7. so far/up to now** have been in **8. vain/vane**. What I need, without any **9. doubt/uncertainty,** is a more permanent solution **10. of/to** the problem. Consequently, with this **11. in/on** mind, I've decided to turn over a new **12. leaf/page**. I've started **13. getting/to get** up an hour earlier each morning to go **14. for a run/running 15. in view of/with a view to** keeping fit. The **16. older/oldest** I get, the more I realise the importance of keeping in **17. order/shape**. **18. Considering/Regarding** the way **19. most/the most** of us **20. abuse/misuse** our bodies, it's **21. barely/hardly** surprising that we end up **22. by/with 23. damaging/injuring** our health. The only **24. sensible/sensitive** solution is for us to change our lifestyles while we still have the **25. chance/possibility; 26. or else/otherwise** it's only a **27. matter/question** of time before we have to pay the **28. price/prize**. It's high time **29. to pay/we paid** more attention **30. on/to** safeguarding our health.

Answers

1. to lose
2. by
3. down
4. like/such as
5. However
6. tell
7. so far/up to now
8. vain
9. doubt
10. to
11. in
12. leaf
13. getting/to get
14. for a run/running
15. with a view to

16. older
17. shape
18. Considering
19. most
20. abuse
21. hardly
22. by
23. damaging
24. sensible
25. chance
26. otherwise
27. matter/question
28. price
29. we paid
30. to

1. **At present/Presently** all I have is a 2. **momentary/temporary** 3. **job/work.** 4. **Despite/In spite** of having to work extremely 5. **hard/hardly,** the 6. **salary/wage** I get paid each week is 7. **minimal/minimum** and by the end of each day I'm totally 8. **exhausted/exhaustive.** 9. **Moreover/Nevertheless,** 10. **unless/until** I've found something better, it looks 11. **as if/like** I'll just have to put up with it. In the 12. **meantime/meanwhile,** I'm studying 13. **half/part-**time for a degree. 14. **in view of/with a view to** improving my 15. **prospects/prospectus.** Although I'm an 16. **industrial/industrious** person, what I lack is qualifications. My boss is an 17. **official/officious** person and he's always ordering me around. He 18. **adapts/adopts** the same attitude with my colleagues. 19. **Moral/Morale** 20. **among/between** the staff is extremely low, which is 21. **comprehensive/understandable.** 22. **Although/Despite** all the problems, I 23. **do/make** my best to 24. **collaborate/co-operate.** There's no 25. **point/use** in handing in my notice as I have nowhere else to go.

Answers

1. At present
2. temporary
3. job
4. In spite
5. hard
6. wage
7. minimal
8. exhausted
9. Nevertheless
10. until
11. as if
12. meantime
13. part

14. with a view to
15. prospects
16. industrious
17. officious
18. adopts
19. Morale
20. among
21. understandable
22. Despite
23. do
24. co-operate
25. point

The 1. **weather/whether** in this country is so 2. **unforeseeable/unpre-dictable** that there's no way 3. **of knowing/to know** what to 4. **except/expect**. Yesterday morning, for example, the sky was filled 5. **of/with** clouds and it looked 6. **as though/like** there was going to be a 7. **downfall/downpour**. 8. **Moreover/Nevertheless**, it also seemed highly unlikely that there would be any 9. **chance/opportunity** of 10. **it/them** improving. 11. **Moreover/Nevertheless**, within the space of a couple of hours the sky cleared 12. **out/up** and there wasn't a cloud in 13. **sight/view**. 14. **Instead of/Rather than** go on a sightseeing tour as I'd originally planned, I decided to 15. **pass/spend** the afternoon in the park. I covered my body with suntan lotion to protect myself from the harmful 16. **affects/effects** of the 17. **beams/rays** and 18. **laid/lay** down on the grass. After a while, it got too hot so I sat in the 19. **shade/shadow** of a nearby tree. It was then that I spotted her walking towards me. I 20. **blinked/winked** twice to 21. **assure/ensure** that I wasn't seeing things because she seemed too 22. **incredible/incredulous** to be true. She was so beautiful that I expected her to walk right 23. **passed/past** me. However, to my amazement, she stopped 24. **asking/to ask** me for a light. I invited her to sit down 25. **by/on** my side and we started 26. **chattering/chatting**. It turned 27. **out/up** that we had a lot in common with one 28. **another/other** and we got on like a house 29. **for sale/on fire**. 30. **By/In** no time at all we were on first name 31. **conditions/terms** and I could see myself getting involved 32. **in/with** her. Although I'm usually 33. **shy/timid** with strangers and 34. **by/in** nature rather reserved, she made me 35. **fall/feel** instantly at ease.

Answers

1. weather	13. sight	25. by
2. unpredictable	14. Rather than	26. chatting
3. of knowing	15. spend	27. out
4. expect	16. effects	28. another
5. with	17. rays	29. on fire
6. as though	18. lay	30. In
7. downpour	19. shade	31. terms
8. Moreover	20. blinked	32. with
9. chance/opportunity	21. ensure	33. shy
10. it	22. incredible	34. by
11. Nevertheless	23. past	35. feel
12. up	24. to ask	

1. **According to/In accordance with** the experts, 2. **by/through** living in a polluted city you can 3. **loose/lose** up to ten years of your life. 4. **Moreover/Nevertheless,** 5. **despite/in spite** the 6. **depressed/depressing** statistics, I still prefer living in London 7. **than/to** living in the country. In any case, 8. **due to/thanks to** the nature of my work I don't really have much choice. 9. **Although/Even though** I enjoy 10. **going/to go** to the country for weekend 11. **brakes/breaks,** I get 12. **bored/boring** if I have to stay any longer than that. 13. **At/In** no time at all I find myself at a 14. **loose/lose** end and look forward to 15. **return/returning** home again. The fact of the matter is that I'm used to 16. **live/living** in big cities as I was born and also brought up in one. One of the 17. **disadvantages/drawbacks** is having to 18. **contend/face** with the rush hour, especially if you live on the 19. **outskirts/suburbs.** In London we're 20. **dependant/dependent** on a public transport system that 21. **leaves/lets** a lot to be 22. **desired/wished for.** 23. **Moreover/Nonetheless,** 24. **fares/fees** are always 25. **raising/rising** while the service seems to 26. **degenerate/deteriorate.** It's the 27. **price/prize** you have to pay for living in a city and it clearly causes a 28. **considerable/considerate** amount of hardship. As 29. **far/long** as I'm concerned, the advantages far 30. **outweigh/overbalance** the negative aspects and nobody can persuade me otherwise.

Answers

1. According to	16. living
2. by	17. disadvantages/drawbacks
3. lose	18. contend
4. Nevertheless	19. outskirts
5. despite	20. dependent
6. depressing	21. leaves
7. to	22. desired
8. due to	23. Moreover
9. Although/Even though	24. fares
10. going	25. rising
11. breaks	26. deteriorate
12. bored	27. price
13. In	28. considerable
14. loose	29. far
15. returning	30. outweigh

How often have you walked into an advanced class to be greeted by a group of students with their legs crossed and arms folded, taking a "go on then, amaze me" attitude. And whatever you try to present, the response is "we've done this before". One tactic is to show this type of learner what they do not know in the hope of breaking down this self-imposed barrier.

The use of shock tactics to start off with can be helpful. Instead of attempting a conventional presentation, you might like to consider making use of a **How Much Do You Know About...?** type questionnaire, like the examples presented on the following pages. The students' embarrassment at their poor results will act as a spur to further study and help them to overcome their initial complacency. Moreover, as such questionnaires entail problem-solving, they provide an ideal way of catering for the logical-mathematical intelligence type.

How Much Do You Know About The Tenses? Decide whether the following statements are true or false and give reasons for the choices you make:

1. The Past Simple tense can be used for present time.

2. WILL can be used to express past time.

3. The Present Simple tense can be used for past time.

4. English only has two tense forms.

5. The imperative can be used for invitations.

6. The Present Simple can be used for future time.

7. The following sentences are interchangeable as they have exactly the same meaning:
   He lives in London.
   He's living in London.

8. The following sentences are interchangeable as they have exactly the same meaning:
   I've written a letter this morning.
   I've been writing a letter this morning.

9. The adverb of frequency ALWAYS is never used with the Present Continuous.

10. The least frequently used tense in English is the Pluperfect.

All the statements are true except for numbers seven, eight, nine and ten. To find out the reasons why, take a look at the explanations below:

1. True - "It's time we left."
2. True - "They will be there by now."
3. True - "In he comes and hits me."
4. True - present simple and past simple.
5. True - "Come in and make yourself at home."
6. True - for timetabled future action. "The train leaves at 8.30pm tonight."
7. False - the Present Simple suggests that it is the person's permanent rather than temporary home.
8. False - the Present Perfect Simple indicates that the letter is finished.
9. False - "She's always contradicting me." The use of ALWAYS with the Present Continuous indicates that the action takes place more frequently than is acceptable.
10. False - the name used for the tense is usually the Past Perfect. The least frequently used tenses are probably the Past Perfect Continuous and the Future Perfect Continuous – because they are both such a mouthful we tend to avoid them.

How Much Do You Know About The Passive? Decide whether the following statements are true or false and give reasons for the choices you make:

1. Verbs followed by an object and the plain infinitive in the active take the TO infinitive in the passive.

2. The agent in the passive is always introduced with the preposition BY.

3. Active sentences with two objects have two possible passive forms.

4. There are certain active sentences that cannot be transformed into the passive.

5. About four out of five English passive clauses have no agent.

6. The passive auxiliary is always the verb TO BE.

7. Every language has a passive form.

8. TO BE TIRED is the passive form of TO TIRE.

9. The causative is always formed with the verb TO HAVE followed by an object and the past participle. For example: "Now that I'm going bald, I don't need to have my hair cut so often."

10. The gerund and infinitive both have passive forms.

All the statements are false except for numbers three, four, five and ten. To find out the reasons why, take a look at the explanations below:

1. False. LET can be followed by an object and the plain infinitive in the active but there is no passive form.
2. False. "I am very impressed WITH your standard of English."
3. True. "They gave the patient the kiss of life" has two possible passive forms: The patient was given the kiss of life/The kiss of life was given to the patient.
4. True. "My boss let me leave early" cannot be transformed into the passive without changing the verb.
5. True. In about eighty percent of cases the agent is unnecessary as it is obvious from the context.
6. False. The passive with GET can be found in informal style and in constructions without an agent.
7. Extremely unlikely! How about Tok pidgin or Xhosa?!?!?!?! (And if you know where either of these languages is spoken, you deserve a bonus point!)
8. False. TIRED is an adjective that can be used with a number of different verbs including BE, FEEL, GET and BECOME.
9. False. The verb GET can be used in place of HAVE. "Now that I'm going bald, I don't need to GET my hair cut so often."
10. True. "Nobody likes being made to look ridiculous and nobody wants to be regarded as an idiot."

How Much Do You Know About Relative Clauses? Decide whether the following statements are true or false and give reasons for the choices you make:

1. Non-defining clauses are a feature of written English.

2. The linking word THAT is used in both defining and non-defining clauses.

3. Non-defining clauses are always placed between commas.

4. Defining clauses require linking words – WHO or WHICH, for example.

5. Non-defining clauses require linking words – WHO or WHICH, for example.

6. Non-defining clauses are always placed in the middle of sentences.

7. WHICH is used to refer to things but not persons.

8. WHOSE can be used to refer to things or persons.

9. THAT is never preceded by a preposition.

10. The relative particle THAT is always unstressed.

All the statements are false except for numbers eight, nine and ten. To find out the reasons, take a look at the explanations below:

1. False. They can also be found in spoken English: "Michael, you know, the man with no hair, works as a language teacher."
2. False. THAT is not used in non-defining clauses.
3. False. They can also be placed between dashes or in brackets.
4. False. "She's the woman I met at the party on Saturday."
5. False. "Buckingham Palace, situated in Central London, is the main residence of the Queen of England."
6. False. They can also be found at the end of sentences: "He's an insomniac, which means he has difficulty in getting to sleep."
7. False. It can be used to refer to persons when a description or classification is intended: "He looked like an estate agent, which he was."
8. True. The only consonants whose notation requires special notice are the following.
9. True. However, it can open a clause with a preposition at the end: "She's the woman that he's been looking for."
10. True.

How Much Do You Know About The Articles? Decide whether the following statements are true or false and give reasons for the choices you make:

1. There are no articles in Korean, Russian, Polish and Japanese.

2. Titles such as MR are never preceded by the indefinite article.

3. Nouns are either countable or uncountable but never both.

4. Words starting with a consonant are never preceded by the indefinite article AN.

5. Both the indefinite and the definite article are among the ten most frequently used words in English.

6. Nouns that are uncountable in English are often countable in other languages.

7. There are three articles in English - A, AN and THE.

8. The names of English newspapers are always preceded by the definite article.

9. The names of English magazines are never preceded by the definite article.

10. Only three names of countries are preceded by the definite article – the USA, the CIS and the UK.

All the statements are false except for numbers one, five and six. To find out the reasons, take a look at the explanations below:

1. True.
2. False. The indefinite article can precede the title MR to indicate that the person is unknown to the speaker: "I met a Mr Brown at the party last night."
3. False. WOOD (uncountable) is a material and A WOOD is a small forest.
4. False. HONEST starts with a consonant but the H is not pronounced. That is why we would say "an honest person".
5. True.
6. True. FURNITURE and ADVICE are uncountable in English but countable in French, Italian, Spanish and Portuguese.
7. False. What about the zero article?!?!?!
8. False. How about "Independent" or "Today" and local papers?
9. False. What about THE ECONOMIST?
10. False. How about the UAE or The Netherlands?

There is no reason why "How much do you know about...?" questionnaires need to be grammar-based. The final example is topic-based and can be used as a lead-in to work on the theme of "Relationships".

How Much Do You Know About Marriage? (Comparison)
Read the following statements and decide if they are true or false:

1. Four out of ten marriages in the UK are likely to end in divorce.

2. Divorce is bad for your health! Divorced men have a greater chance of dying prematurely than married men.

3. Admission rates to mental hospitals are higher among the divorced than the married.

4. Research shows that divorced people smoke more, drink more and eat more.

5. A higher percentage of divorced people commit suicide than single people.

6. Women are keener than men on divorce.

7. More divorced men live to regret their decision to get divorced than women.

8. By law, no divorced member of the British monarchy is allowed to ascend the throne.

9. It is a tradition for brides to wear "something old, something new, something borrowed and something in the shoe".

10. Two witnesses are required at a marriage ceremony to make it legal.

All the statements are true except for numbers four, eight and nine. To find out the reasons, take a look at the explanations below:

1. True.
2. True. Divorced men aged twenty-five to forty are twice as likely as married men to die prematurely.
3. True. Admission rates are between four and six times greater among the divorced than the married.
4. False. Divorced people smoke more and drink more but there is no evidence to suggest they eat more too. However, research indicates that divorced people also have higher rates of unsafe sex.
5. True. They are four times more likely to commit suicide.
6. True. Seventy percent of petitions are filed by women.
7. True. Fifty-one percent of divorced men live to regret it, saying they would have preferred to stay married, compared with twenty - nine percent of women.
8. False. However, no member of the Roman Catholic Church is allowed to ascend the throne.
9. False. The tradition is for the bride to wear "something old, something new, something borrowed and something blue".
10. True.

A traditional aid to learning, which can still be helpful, is the use of mnemonic devices. Some of you can probably remember learning at school "i before e except after c", for example. Another example of a mnemonic is OPSHACOM to remember the order of adjectives before nouns:

❖ Opinion
❖ Shape
❖ Age
❖ Colour
❖ Origin
❖ Material

However, such devices become even more meaningful when the learners have the opportunity to create their own. This can be provided in the review stage of a lesson.

Unit 6: How To Cater For Linguistic Intelligence

Students who seem to mirror the learning styles of teachers, who display a fascination for words and their manipulation, who enjoy expressing themselves orally and in writing as well as listening to stories are likely to have well-developed linguistic intelligence. Storytelling provides the ideal means of catering for these students in class, and this is the main focus of this unit.

We often assume we know what is best for students without bothering to find out what they really want. That is why there is a strong case to be made for having a "round" at the end of each week – a feedback session to find out how they are feeling and what they would like more or less of. You have every right to participate in this process too and to share your own feelings with the group. After these reflections, a programme can be planned for the following week taking everyone's views into account.

A point that is likely to be raised in such a session is that the learners appreciate having the opportunity to listen to good examples of authentic English. In our attempts to reduce Teacher Talking Time, we tend to overlook this and put the emphasis on the students doing all the talking. One way of taking their wishes into account is through the use of storytelling. However, this does not have to be a passive experience for the learners as the material presented below will illustrate.

Whenever people meet, stories are told and they have been told since time immemorial. Storytelling is an oral tradition and because of the issues which have been worked through by means of the stories, storytelling has contributed to the creation of the great epics of the world. The earliest stories were probably chants or songs of praise for the natural world in pagan times. Later, dance and music accompanied the stories. The storyteller would become the entertainer for the community and the historian, musician and poet too. The oral tales that were passed on from one generation to the next by word of mouth included myths, parables, fables, fairy tales and folk tales.

It is helpful to draw a distinction between the telling and the reading of stories. The former is much more likely to hold the attention of the audience and have a greater impact. Moreover, in the language-teaching classroom, you can adapt the story to cater for the level of your students by telling it instead of reading it.

There is a strong case to be made for not pre-teaching new vocabulary when storytelling unless it is absolutely essential for the enjoyment of the tale. Stories are above all for enjoyment. As teachers of English we want to exploit them for language purposes, but we must take care not to milk them dry and kill the joy. Dealing with new vocabulary as it arises gives you the chance to present it in context, elicit its meaning, and then give the students the opportunity to transfer it to another setting. It helps to break the story up into more manageable chunks and enables you to involve the class more actively in the storytelling process. Moreover, a few words unknown to the reader can add effectiveness and local colour to a narrative.

As a post-reading activity, you can cut up the stories into paragraphs for the students, working in groups, to put in order. Another possibility is to omit the ending of the story when telling it to the class, then to invite the learners, again in in groups, to predict the conclusion. After listening to the various suggestions they come up with, students can compare their suggestions with the original ending which you can display on an overhead transparency.

In *Implementing The Lexical Approach* (1997) Michael Lewis suggests an activity that can be used with whatever story you tell. Instead of providing the learners with a set of questions based on the text, the students are invited to produce their own. An adapted version of the idea is presented below.

Work in pairs. Prepare a set of questions about the story. Then exchange your questions with another pair and answer the questions you receive. Use the following frames to help you:

a. What did you think was the most ... thing about the story?

b. Was there anything in the story that really ... you?

c. According to the story, what ... ?

d. What reasons are given for ... ?

e. In what way would ... ?

f. Do you agree with the ideas/suggestion that ... ?

◆ Another activity that could be used to follow any story was suggested to me by John Morgan, teacher-trainer at Pilgrims. The idea is to go round the class and to ask everyone to offer one line from a story they know. Then go round the class a second time, asking the students to add a second line to the first line from their tales. The students can then be invited to go over to the person whose lines they found the most interesting and listen to the whole story the original extract came from. It is a gentle and non-threatening way of encouraging the learners to tell tales to each other without being under the pressure of having to tell a story to the group as a whole. While the tales are being exchanged, you can circulate and make a note of any errors that crop up on an overhead transparency. This can be flashed up on the board at the end of the activity and the students can be given the opportunity to self-correct.

◆ An alternative way of making use of the learners' own stories is to invite some of the students to tell you a story about themselves outside class time. Then you write up the story for them, sticking as closely as possible to the original, but making sure that it's readable and the English is correct. It is a great boost to the person's confidence to see a story of their own in correct English shared with the class. It might even be possible for the storyteller, with some prior preparation, to run the lesson in your place.

◆ Story cards can be created to facilitate storytelling too. Twenty cards can be cut out and divided into five categories – characters, events, actions, times and places. Draw a picture with a caption on each of the cards and mark the category on the back. To play the game, invite the students to choose one card from each category and then to prepare a story based on the prompts on the cards. Although games like this take a great deal of preparation, they can be recycled and are well worth the time and effort required.

One of the justifications for the use of storytelling in the classroom is its global nature as an activity. Students are not restricted to a narrow range of potential language as can happen with grammar-focused coursebook activities. There is the opportunity to draw upon all areas of their previous knowledge of the language as well as to experiment with new forms.

Reading, listening to tales, the students presenting their own stories, and wordbuilding games all cater for linguistic intelligence so the lesson plans presented below provide an ideal means of catering for this particular intelligence type in class. *Connla And The Fairy Maiden* is intended for an Advanced level class whereas *Bedd Gelert* is appropriate for Intermediate level students.

Connla And The Fairy Maiden

Connla of the Fiery Hair was son of Conn of the Hundred Fights. One day as he stood by the side of his father on the height of Usna, he saw a maiden clad in strange attire coming towards him.

"Whence comest thou, maiden?" said Connla.

"I come from the Plains of the Ever-Living," she said. "There where there is neither death nor sin. There we keep holiday alway, nor need we help from any in our joy. And in all our pleasure we have no strife. And because we have our homes in the round green hills, men call us the Hill Folk."

The king and all with him wondered much to hear a voice when they saw no one. For save Connla alone, none saw the Fairy Maiden.

"To whom art thou talking, my son?" said Conn the King.

Then the maiden answered, "Connla speaks to a young, fair maid, whom neither death nor old age awaits. I love Connla, and now I call him away to the Plain of Pleasure, Moy Mell, where Boadag is King for aye, nor has there been complaint or sorrow in that land since he has held the kingship. Oh, come with me, Connla of the Fiery Hair, ruddy as the dawn with thy tawny skin. A fairy crown awaits thee to grace thy comely face and royal form. Come, and never shall thy comeliness fade, nor thy youth, till the last awful day of judgment."

The king, in fear of what the maiden said, which he heard though he could not see her, called aloud to his Druid, Coran by name.

"Oh, Coran of the Many Spells," he said, "and of the Cunning Magic, I call upon thy aid. A task is upon me too great for all my skill and wit, greater than any laid upon me since I seized the kingship. A maiden unseen has met us, and by her power would take from me my dear, my comely son. If thou help not, he will be taken from thy king by woman's wiles and witchery."

Then Coran the Druid stood forth and chanted his spells towards the spot where the maiden's voice had been heard. And none heard her voice again, nor could Connla see her longer. Only, as she vanished before the Druid's mighty spell, she threw an apple to Connla.

For a whole month from that day Connla would take nothing, either to eat or to drink, save only from that apple. But as he ate it grew again and always kept whole. And all the while there grew within him a mighty yearning and longing after the maiden he had seen.

But when the last day of the month of waiting came, Connla stood by the side of the king his father on the Plain of Arcomin, and again he saw the maiden come towards him, and again she spoke to him.

"Tis a glorious place, forsooth, that Connla holds among short-lived mortals awaiting the day of death. But now the folk of life, the ever-living ones, beg and bid thee come to Moy Mell, the Plain of Pleasure, for they have learnt to know thee, seeing thee in thy home among thy dear ones."

When Conn the king heard the maiden's voice he called to his men aloud and said:

"Summon swift my Druid Coran, for I see she has again this day the power of speech."

Then the maiden said: "Oh, mighty Conn, fighter of a hundred fights, the Druid's power is little loved; it has little honour in the mighty land, peopled with so many of the upright. When the Law will come, it will do away with the Druid's magic spells that came from the lips of the false black demon."

Then Conn the king observed that since the maiden came Connla his son spoke to none that spake to him. So Conn of the Hundred Fights said to him: "It is to thy mind what the woman says, my son?"

"Tis hard upon me," then said Connla. "I loved my own folk above all things; but yet, but yet a longing seizes me for the maiden."

When the maiden heard this, she answered and said: "The ocean is not so strong as the waves of thy longing. Come with me in my curragh, the gleaming, straight-gliding crystal canoe. Soon we can reach Boadag's realm. I see the bright sun sink, yet far as it is, we can reach it before dark. There is, too, another land worthy of thy journey, a land joyous to all that seek it. Only wives and maidens dwell there. If thou wilt, we can seek it and live there alone together in joy."

When the maiden ceased to speak, Connla of the Fiery Hair rushed away from them and sprang into the curragh, the gleaming, straight-gliding crystal canoe. And then they all, king and court, saw it glide away over the bright sea towards the setting sun. Away and away, till eye could see it no longer, and Connla and the Fairy Maiden went their way on the sea, and were no more seen, nor did any know where they came.

(taken from *Celtic Fairy Tales*, collected by Joseph Jacobs, 1968)

1. *Elicit what a 'fairy' is from the class, then brainstorm what the students associate fairies with and board the language that comes up in the form of a mind map. A mind map is a non-linear form of note taking which links key words and ideas. In its simplest form, it could consist of the word FAIRIES inside a circle in the centre of the board, with arrows radiating from the circumference pointing to key vocabulary. An alternative would be to stick up a picture of a fairy in the centre of the board.*

2. *Ask the class what stories they know about fairies.*

   The following story is a traditional Celtic tale about the power that fairies can have over people.

3. *Narrate the story.*

4. *Pause after Connla is given the apple. Ask the class to predict what follows:* What do you think happens to Connla after he eats the apple? And what story does this remind you of?

5. *Pause after "Is it to thy mind what the woman says, my son?" Ask the students to predict what follows:* What do you think Connla is going to do - stay with his own folk or follow the Fairy Maiden? What would you do in his place?

6. What do you think happens to Connla when he reaches the Plains of the Ever Living? Working in small groups, see if you can continue the story and bring it to a conclusion.

7. *Arrange the students in groups of three to work on the following role-play:*

   Connla – torn between staying with his father or following the Fairy.
   Conn the King – eager to persuade his son to stay with his own folk.
   The Fairy Maiden – eager to persuade Connla to join her.

Give the learners a few minutes to plan what they are going to say, before acting out the situation. Circulate from group to group, to make a note of any problems that crop up which you can then deal with at the end of the session.

HEART IDIOMS
HEART IDIOMS Match the idioms on the left with the explanations on the right. There are more explanations than idioms so make sure you select the correct ones!

1. You're a man after my own heart.

2. I see you've had a change of heart.

3. My heart goes out to you.

4. You've got a heart of stone.

5. Please don't lose heart.

6. You clearly put your heart and soul in it.

7. You've clearly set your heart on it.

8. The trouble with you is that you wear your heart on your sleeve.

9. I feel your heart's just not in it.

10. I know you've got my best interests at heart.

a. Don't become discouraged.

b. Don't stop loving me.

c. I can see you tried very hard.

d. I feel you genuinely care about me.

e. I know you're determined to let nothing stand in your way.

f. I love you from a distance.

g. It's clear you no longer feel the same way.

h. We have the same tastes.

i. We both love the same person.

j. You can't hide your feelings.

k. You can't show your feelings.

l. You don't seem to be well motivated.

m. You don't seem to have any feelings.

n. You have my sympathy.

Answers

1-h
2-g
3-n
4-m
5-a
6-c
7-e
8-j
9-l
10-d

Bedd Gelert

Prince Llewelyn had a favourite greyhound named Gelert that had been given to him by his father-in-law, King John. He was as gentle as a lamb at home but a lion in the chase. One day Llewelyn went to the chase and blew his horn in front of his castle. All his other dogs came to the call but Gelert never answered it. So he blew a louder blast on his horn and called Gelert by name, but still the greyhound did not come. At last Prince Llewelyn could wait no longer and went off to the hunt without Gelert. He had little sport that day because Gelert was not there, the swiftest and boldest of his hounds.

He turned back in a rage to his castle, and as he came to the gate, who should he see but Gelert come bounding out to meet him. But when the hound came near him, the Prince was startled to see that his lips and fangs were dripping with blood. Llewelyn started back and the greyhound crouched down at his feet as if surprised or afraid at the way his master greeted him.

Now Prince Llewelyn had a little son a year old with whom Gelert used to play, and a terrible thought crossed the Prince's mind that made him rush towards the child's nursery. And the nearer he came the more blood and disorder he found about the rooms. He rushed into the nursery and found the child's cradle overturned and daubed with blood.

Prince Llewelyn grew more and more terrified, and sought for his little son everywhere. He could find him nowhere but only signs of some terrible conflict in which much blood had been shed. At last he felt sure the dog had destroyed his child, and, shouting to Gelert: "Monster, thou hast devoured my child," he drew out his sword and plunged it into the greyhound's side, who fell with a deep yell and still gazing into his master's eyes.

As Gelert raised his dying yell, a little child's cry answered it from beneath the cradle, and there Llewelyn found his child unharmed and just awakened from sleep. But just beside him lay the body of a great gaunt wolf all torn to pieces and covered with blood. Too late, Llewelyn learned what had happened while he was away. Gelert had stayed behind to guard the child and had fought and slain the wolf that had tried to destroy Llewelyn's heir.

In vain was all Llewelyn's grief; he could not bring his faithful dog to life again. So he buried him outside the castle walls within sight of the great mountain of Snowdon, where every passer-by might see his grave, and raised over it a great cairn of stones. And to this day the place is called Bedd Gelert, or the Grave of Gelert.

(taken from *Celtic Fairy Tales*, collected by Joseph Jacobs, 1968)

1. They say that a dog is a man's best friend. What feelings do you have towards dogs?

Near Mount Snowdon in Wales you can visit the grave of a dog called Gelert and here's the story of what happened to him.

2. *Narrate the story.*

3. *Pause after* "He had little sport that day because Gelert was not there, the swiftest and boldest of the hounds." *Ask the students to predict what follows:* Why do you think Gelert failed to answer the call?

4. Pause after "Too late, Llewelyn learned what had happened while he was away". *Ask the class to predict what follows:* What do you think had happened while Prince Llewelyn was away?

5. *Pause after* "he could not bring his faithful dog to life again". *Ask the students to predict the ending:* What do you think Llewelyn did to make amends for his mistake?

6. Have you ever acted in haste, then regretted it later? Tell me about it.

7. The storyteller says Gelert was **as gentle as a lamb**. How many of the following animal similes do you know? There are thirteen animals and twelve spaces. Which animal does not fit?

a bat / a bee/ a bird / a dog / an eel / a fox / a kitten / a lion / a mouse / an owl / a mule / a peacock / a pig

a. as blind as ...
b. as brave as ...
c. as busy as ...
d. as cunning as ...
e. as free as ...

f. as obstinate as ...
g. as playful as ...
h. as proud as ...
i. as quiet as ...
j. as slippery as ...

Dog Idioms Match the idioms on the left with the explanations on the right. There are more explanations than you need so make sure you select the correct ones!

1. Why are you dressed up like a dog's dinner?

2. Why don't you let sleeping dogs lie?

3. There's life in the old dog yet so stop trying to write me off!

4. I'm top dog in this office so be careful what you say.

5. I'm in the doghouse because I forgot my girlfriend's birthday.

6. You can't teach an old dog new tricks.

7. Every dog has his day.

8. It's a dog's life.

9. You don't stand a dog's chance.

10. I made a dog's dinner of the job.

11. Don't be such a dog in the manger.

12. You'll find my bark is worse than my bite.

a. Don't look for trouble intentionally.

b. I'm angry.

c. I'm in trouble.

d. I'm not the monster I seem to be.

e. I'm still fit and active.

f. I'm the boss.

g. I did everything right.

h. I did everything wrong.

i. It's an easy life for some people.

j. People who are set in their ways find it hard to adapt.

k. There's nothing but trouble and misery.

l. We all have our problems.

m. Why are you trying so hard to impress?

n. Why do you look so untidy?

o. Why try to stop people enjoying themselves?

p. You can have no hope of success.

q. You have every chance of success.

r. Your chance will come.

Answers

1-m	7-r
2-a	8-k
3-e	9-p
4-f	10-h
5-c	11-o
6-j	12-d

The following ballad could be set to music and used for follow-up work on the tale. The unit on **How To Cater For Musical Intelligence** has suggestions for exploiting songs, and the final verse could be used as a chorus.

The Ballad Of Gelert

Gelert was a brave dog
Courageous, loyal and true
And for his master Llewelyn
There was nothing he would not do

One day the Prince went hunting
But Gelert stayed at home
For he'd had a premonition
Not to leave Llewelyn's son alone

And he was right to follow his instincts
For while the baby slept
A fox crept into the nursery
But Gelert lay in wait

When Llewelyn returned he looked for his son
But he was nowhere to be seen
All he found was Gelert covered in blood
So concluded he was to blame

In a rage Llewelyn drew his sword
And sliced off Gelert's head
Too late, too late he noticed his son
And realised his mistake

What had he done, what had he done
Killed the dog who'd saved his son's life
No power on earth could bring him back
So he built a monument to him instead

And if you travel to the North of Wales
The monument you will see
In memory of Gelert
A braver dog there will never be

Gelert, brave Gelert
You did not die in vain
For your tale will be handed down
And long will we remember your name.

Acrostics, such as the topic-based examples presented below, cater for linguistic intelligence and will appeal to those learners who display a fascination for words. At higher levels the students can be encouraged to make their own versions to try out on each other.

Answer the clues across to complete the grid:

1. There isn't enough room in this flat to swing a ... !
2. An Englishman's home is his ... .
3. ... begins at home.
4. As safe as ... .
5. Wherever you go, there's no place like ... .
6. You can talk until the cows ... home but it won't make the least bit of difference.
7. People who live in glasshouses shouldn't throw ... .
8. Before you criticise others, you should put your own house in ... .
9. Home is where your ... is.
10. Although it's supposed to be a five-star hotel, it's nothing to ... home about.
11. We took to each other the moment we met and we got on like a house on ... .
12. If my parents find out that I've been seeing you behind their backs, they'll hit the ... .
13. When poverty comes in at the door, love flies out of the ... .

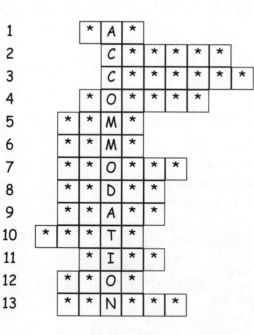

(Answers on next page)

Answer the clues across to complete the grid:

1. Are you ... me of being a liar?
2. What a policeman wears.
3. It took the jury a long time to reach a ... .
4. Although I was ... for causing the accident, it wasn't my fault.
5. The murderer was ... to life imprisonment.
6. You shouldn't steal. It's ... the law.
7. Someone who gives evidence in court.
8. The person who decides what the punishment should be.
9. A dead body.
10. Someone who takes goods illegally from one country into another.
11. The opposite of GUILTY.
12. She was so depressed that she tried to commit ... .
13. What 7. does in court.
14. The motorist was taken to the police station and ... with exceeding the speed limit.
15. Anyone who commits a crime.
16. In court you have to ... to tell the truth.
17. If the traffic warden gives you a ticket, you'll have to pay a ... .
18. " ... is the best policy"

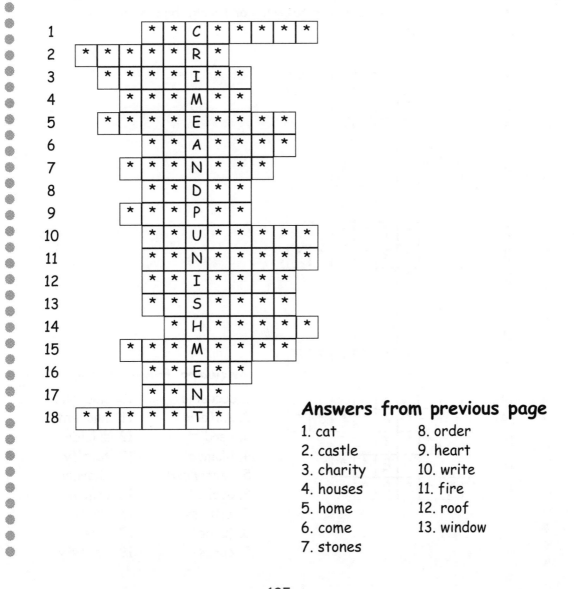

Answers from previous page

1. cat
2. castle
3. charity
4. houses
5. home
6. come
7. stones
8. order
9. heart
10. write
11. fire
12. roof
13. window

Answer the clues across to complete the grid:

1. It's the most beautiful place I've ever visited – it's like ... on earth.
2. Tribal peoples are being wiped off the ... of the earth by so-called civilised man.
3. I'd move heaven and ... just for the chance to be with you again!
4. The clothes in that department store ... the earth. If I were you, I'd shop somewhere else.
5. What's the matter with you? You look like ... on earth!
6. If you took the job with that rival company, it would be like jumping out of the ... pan into the fire.
7. Don't play with me because you're playing ... fire.
8. I'd go ... fire and water to help a friend in need.
9. There's no ... without fire.
10. The only way to ... the air is by talking.
11. I don't know where he's gone – he just disappeared into ... air.
12. I can't stand people who put on airs and ... . Why can't they just be themselves?
13. A lot of water has ... under the bridge since the last time we met.
14. The delicious smell coming from the kitchen is ... my mouth water.
15. If the authorities find out what she's done, she'll be in ... water.
16. You can ... a horse to water but you can't make him drink.
17. Still ... run deep.

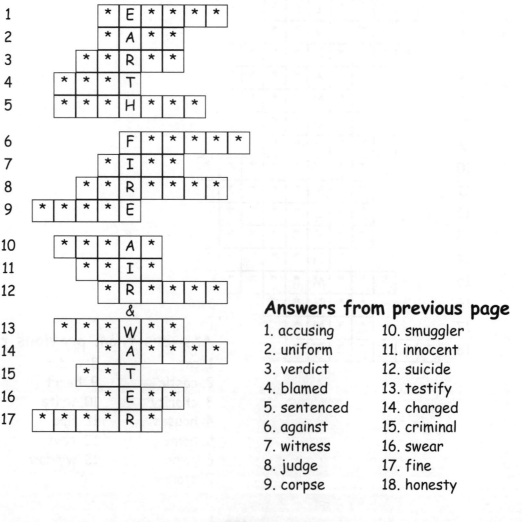

Answers from previous page

1. accusing	10. smuggler
2. uniform	11. innocent
3. verdict	12. suicide
4. blamed	13. testify
5. sentenced	14. charged
6. against	15. criminal
7. witness	16. swear
8. judge	17. fine
9. corpse	18. honesty

Answers from previous page

1. heaven
2. face
3. earth
4. cost
5. nothing
6. frying
7. with
8. through
9. smoke
10. clear
11. thin
12. graces
13. flowed
14. making
15. hot
16. lead
17. waters

There are many different types of word games that can be employed in the classroom and the **Snake Shapes** presented below offer further examples:

Snake Shapes Answer the clues **across** and **down** to complete the grid:

Across

1. You ... my back and I'll ... yours.
3. The other candidates for the job have more experience than you so I can't say I fancy your ... .
4. We've been arguing with each other for far too long and it's time we buried the ... .
6. There's no time like the ... .
7. Horror films send ... down my spine.
9. He who laughs last, laughs ... .

Down

2. You shouldn't take the law into your own ... .
3. Don't go out without a coat in this weather or you'll ... your death of cold.
5. I'm in a bit of a ... spot because I'm afraid I can't pay the bill.
6. It never rains but it ... .
8. To cut a long story ... , they all lived happily ever after.

Answers from previous page

Across
1. scratch
3. chances
4. hatchet
6. present
7. shivers
9. longest

Down
2. hands
3. catch
5. tight
6. pours
8. short

Snake Shapes Answer the clues **across** and **down** to complete the grid:

Across

1. The only way I managed to pass the exam was by learning everything parrot ... .
3. Red sky at night shepherd's ... .
4. Lightning never ... in the same place twice.
6. As ... as Punch.
7. I'm afraid you let the opportunity slip through your ... .
9. It's time we both agreed to ... and forget.

Down

2. We decided to make a ... of it by going out for dinner and then seeing a late film.
3. It's impossible to know what went on at the meeting behind closed ... .
5. More haste, less ... .
6. The ... of the pudding is in the eating.
8. I'm tired and I could do with a breathing ... .

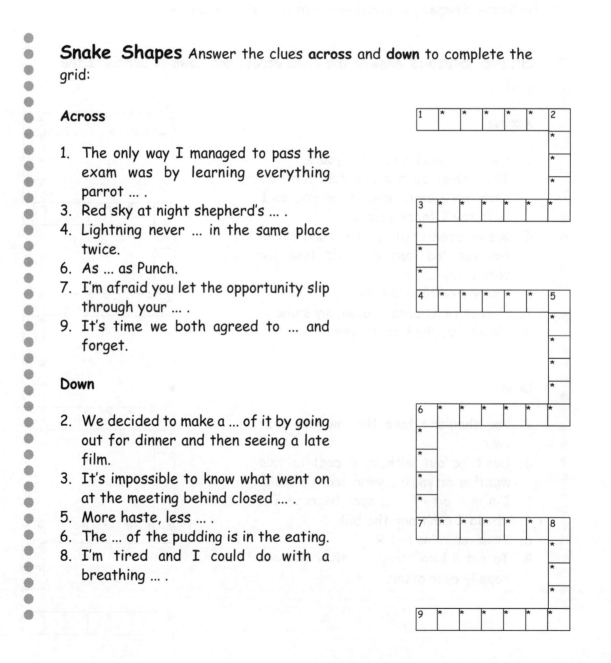

Answers from previous page

Across
1. fashion
3. delight
4. strikes
6. pleased
7. fingers
9. forgive

Down
2. night
3. doors
5. speed
6. proof
8. space

Snake Shapes Answer the clues **across** and **down** to complete the grid:

Across

1. Experience is the best ... .
3. I'm afraid I forgot all about it – it ... my mind.
4. Prices have ... rock bottom so now is not the time to sell.
6. ... is golden.
7. If you're feeling under the ... , why don't you take the day off work?
9. ... can't be choosers.

Down

2. I don't think you're suited to the job – you're like a square peg in a ... hole.
3. As ... as a judge.
5. There's been a great song and ... in the newspapers about the latest scandal to hit the Royal Family.
6. It's the last ... that breaks the camel's back.
8. All ... lead to Rome.

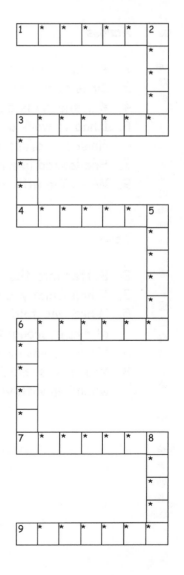

Answers from previous page

Across
1. teacher
3. slipped
4. reached
6. silence
7. weather
9. beggars

Down
2. round
3. sober
5. dance
6. straw
8. roads

Snake Shapes Answer the clues **across** and **down** to complete the grid:

Across

1. A bad ... always blames his tools.
3. Birds of a ... flock together.
4. A ... shared is a ... halved.
6. I had to work at full ... to get the job finished before the end of the week.
7. She looked like mutton ... up as lamb.
9. When I'm with you I'm in ... heaven!

Down

2. Better late than ... .
3. When I met you it was love at ... sight.
5. When you told me what you thought of me, it brought me back down to ... .
6. Horror films make my hair ... on end.
8. You know so much more than I do that when I'm with you I feel out of my ...

   .

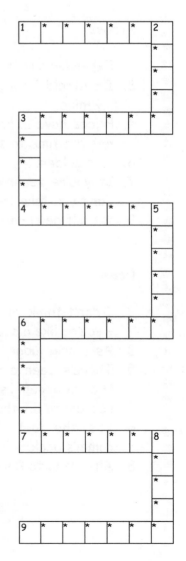

Answers from previous page

Across
1. workman
3. feather
4. trouble
6. stretch
7. dressed
9. seventh

Down
2. never
3. first
5. earth
6. stand
8. depth

Snake Shapes

Answer the clues **across** and **down** to complete the grid:

Across

1. One man's meat is ... man's poison.
3. You don't know what you're talking about – you're talking ... the top of your hat.
4. ... is the best policy.
6. The spirit is ... but the flesh is weak.
7. I wish you wouldn't take me for ... and you'd show some appreciation for a change.
9. I wasn't expecting you to do that – I'm afraid you caught me ... .

Down

2. You have to learn to take the ... with the smooth.
3. I'm fed up to the back ... with you!
5. You're only ... once.
6. I'm afraid you've got hold of the ... end of the stick and completely misunderstood me.
8. I'm absolutely starving and ... for something to eat.

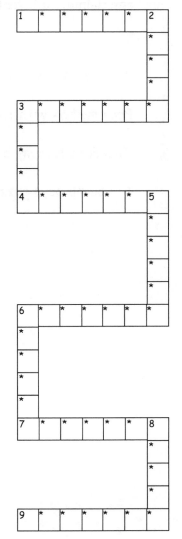

Answers from previous page

Across
1. another
3. through
4. honesty
6. willing
7. granted
9. napping

Down
2. rough
3. teeth
5. young
6. wrong
8. dying

To conclude this section on catering for linguistic intelligence, how about some work on **pangrams**? Pangrams are sentences and phrases using the entire alphabet. *The quick brown fox jumps over a lazy dog*, for example. As a warmer while waiting for late arrivals or if you have a few minutes to spare at the end of a lesson, you can arrange the students in groups to produce pangrams of their own. You could start by eliciting what a *pangram* is by showing the class some examples and prizes could be awarded for the most entertaining or inventive results. Here are some more samples of the form:

The five boxing wizards jump quickly

Pack my box with five dozen liquor jugs

Jackdaws love my big sphinx of quartz

Six plump boys guzzling cheap raw vodka quite joyfully

Unit 7: How to Cater For Spatial Intelligence

Students with a high degree of spatial intelligence tend to think in pictures, are comfortable with maps, charts and diagrams, enjoy drawing and/or doodling, and are likely to make use of coloured markers. Visual problem-solving devices such as spider diagrams, memory maps, and the use of peripherals placed at or higher than eye-level will have a significant impact on such learners.

Guided visualisation can also be used to good effect to cater for spatial intelligence in the classroom. Contrary to what you might expect, there is nothing new about the use of guided visualisation, guided fantasies, creative visualisation or "inner journeying" as it sometimes called. In fact, the technique can be traced back thousands of years to shamanic practices in pagan times.

In tribal societies, when people had physical, emotional or spiritual problems, they would turn to the Shaman or Medicine Man/Woman. (S)He would then journey into what Carlos Castaneda calls "non-ordinary reality" to find solutions to the people's problems. The altered state of consciousness was accessed through drumming, fasting, dancing or by taking psychoactive drugs. More recently the same technique has been employed in psychotherapy by practitioners of psychosynthesis and in Neuro-Linguistic Programming, and it is now being introduced into the classroom for the first time.

The words "hypnosis" and "trance" have negative connotations for some people. However, "hypnosis" is only a word to describe the tools you can use to systematically take someone into an altered state of consciousness. People enter altered states all the time. A good example of this would be daydreaming, something we all do at one time or another and something which is perfectly natural. In fact, not being able to daydream is much more likely to be a cause for concern. Another instance of being in an altered state of consciousness is the time we spend sleeping – on average eight hours a night, one third of

our lives. Nobody can be hypnotised without their consent and nobody can be made to do something which conflicts with their values and beliefs.

So what is guided visualisation? Basically, it involves creating pictures in your mind while following a script. Although the form of the "journey" is controlled by the script, the content remains unpredictable. It is a means of moving what Carlos Castaneda (the developer of the Suggestopedic approach) calls "the assemblage point" and of entering a state of non-ordinary reality.

Why use guided visualisation in the classroom? Firstly, to introduce variety. The wider the choice of activities used, the more likely we are to hold the students' attention and the more likely we are to provide memorable experiences for the learners. Another good reason for using the technique is that it allows the students to express their creativity and uniqueness. Moreover, to keep the brain in a wide-open, unfocused state and to facilitate learning, there must be relaxation and deflection of conscious attention to tasks other than the real goal. Guided visualisation is clearly a means of achieving this.

Psychological research indicates that people become less inhibited in trance-like states, under hypnosis for example. The state induced in the case of guided visualisation is an extremely light trance but the effect is the same on the learners, and the language they produce seems to flow more freely than usual. Another advantage of inducing a trance state is that stimuli can bypass our critical evaluation system and move directly into long-term memory storage.

Are there any dangers involved in using guided visualisation in the classroom and how can they be avoided? Although the majority of people have no difficulty in visualising, a small percentage will find it a problem. However, even these people can describe what they feel, hear, taste or smell on their journeys. It may also be argued that this is the kind of activity that learners either love or hate and it is consequently risky to use in the classroom. This probably depends to a large extent on the atmosphere the teacher succeeds in creating and how the activity is introduced and presented. Our students deserve to be treated with respect, the same respect we would expect from them. They are entitled to explanations as to why we choose to use certain techniques, the reasoning behind the choices we make. Another possible danger is that visualisations can unearth personal issues which cannot be dealt with in the classroom is not the place to deal with. However, the likelihood of this happening is very limited as the visualisations are controlled and directed towards particular aims.

People are most receptive to right-brain insights when the body is relaxed and the mind free from internal chatter. Moreover, brain research confirms that as stress increases, the ability to learn decreases, so establishing the right kind of atmosphere is clearly crucial. It is suggested that the scripts are read with musical accompa-niment to help produce conditions conducive to optimum learning. You can make use of the Baroque music that Dr Lozanov (a Bulgarian psychotherapist in the 1970s) recommends for the Passive Concert in the Suggestopedic cycle. This includes *Concerti Grossi, op.* 6, No. 4, 10, 11, 12 by Corelli and *Five Concerti for Flute and Chamber Orchestra* (G Major, F Major, G Minor, C Major) by Vivaldi. The beat per second paces the brain into a slower frequency alpha range of seven to eleven cycles per second.

As a lead-in to each visualisation, you might like to brainstorm the topic to find out how much the students already know – what they know about the Loch Ness Monster, for example. A certain amount of pre-teaching of new vocabulary might be necessary to ensure the success of the activity. This clearly depends on the level of the class. An alternative to conventional pre-teaching could be to use the first stage of the Suggestopedic cycle. This would entail preparing the classroom before the students arrive – with visuals related to the topic on the walls, music associated with the theme playing on the cassette recorder to greet the class, and realia placed on the floor or on a table in the middle of the room. When the students enter the classroom, they can pick up the realia and start talking about it together.

As outer images tend to overwhelm inner imagery, most people find it easier to visualise when sensory stimulation is reduced. That is why closing the eyes or wearing a blindfold is recommended. However, it is perfectly possible to learn to image with the eyes open if the participants feel more comfortable that way. It is also advisable not to cross your legs or fold your arms while visualising so as to remain open to the process.

It should be pointed out that not everyone will be willing to share their experiences with the group, especially if they are relatively new arrivals. If this turns out to be the case, there is clearly no point in forcing them to do so. As a follow-up to the visualisation, the students can be invited to produce a piece of creative writing based on their experiences. Those members of the group who were reluctant to share their journeys with their classmates will probably feel more at ease when it comes to writing about them and in this way they will still have the opportunity to take part in the process.

Other forms of follow-up work could include drawing, painting, dancing, or singing. Galyean points out that "expressing and communicating are ways of imprinting the information in our memories. It helps to follow imagery work with a verbal and/or nonverbal mode of expressing what we've experienced". Eric Jensen, in his book **Brain Based Learning and Teaching** (1995), makes the point that humans never really cognitively understand or learn something until they can create a personal metaphor or model. Using a creative visualisation to realise the topic in their imagination is one way of achieving this.

A graceful way of guiding someone into a trance state is by making use of transitional words like "as" or "when" – words which imply there is a meaningful relationship between two utterances or events. Imagine, for example, you are reading a script and are interrupted by the sound of a police siren wailing in the street outside. You could improvise and incorporate this into the script: "And as you hear the sound of the siren wailing, it takes you deeper and deeper into the trance."

Before writing a script, decide on your setting and then list the things you would see, hear, feel, smell and taste in the location. The ideal script will include as many different VAKOG elements as possible – to cater for the visual, auditory, kinesthetic, olfactory and gustatory sensory modes. Everyone has a preference for a particular mode, and if you omit one, you could be leaving out the one someone really needs in order to be able to get the most out of the experience.

This is not the only reason for involving all the sensory modes. As a result of recently acquired knowledge of how the brain works, we now know that an experience with a powerful attachment to emotions or feelings is more likely to be retained in the long-term memory. By inviting the learners to attune to their feelings during visualisation, we can ensure this has a better chance of taking place.

Another point to remember is that affirmations should be incorporated into the script, both to help the participants to relax and to affirm the students' ability to learn the language easily and well. "And with each stroke of the oars through the water, you feel more and more relaxed," or "And now that you have completed your journey, you can appreciate more than ever how simple English is to understand". The development of self-esteem and self-belief contribute to the physical condition of relaxed alertness which optimises learning and the use of affirmations can help to promote this.

If any of the students seem to be a bit "spaced out" after a guided visualisation, advise them to try stamping their feet on the ground or to breathe out sharply three or four times. Another technique is get them to close their eyes and picture roots emerging from their feet, going deep into the earth. Always check to make sure everyone has "come back" from the journey and is grounded before moving on, especially if it's the end of the class and anyone is driving home.

In the sample scripts for journeys, you will find the following phrase: "You have a minute of clock time, equal to all the time you need... ." It was coined by Dr Jean Houston, director of the Foundation for Mind Research in New York. During an imagery exercise subjective time is experienced. The brain processes millions of images in microseconds, so in one sixty-second period you do have all the time you need.

A Guided Visualisation: The Loch Ness Monster

Script for the guide *(to be read in a gentle, trance-inducing voice)*

Make yourself comfortable and close your eyes. Take a few deep breaths to help you relax. Feel the tension disappear stage by stage from the top of your head to the tips of your toes. Let your surroundings fade away as you gradually sink backwards through time and actuality and pass through the gateway of reality into the dreamtime. (When the participants are fully relaxed, begin the next stage.)

Today's a very special day in your life because you're going to have an experience that very few people have ever had – you're going to have the opportunity to meet Nessie, the Loch Ness Monster. Nessie knows that you have no wish to harm her and so you have nothing to fear.

You're sitting in a small fishing boat close to the shore of the mysterious and fascinating lake. It's early in the morning, so early that the sun has only just risen and you're surrounded by snow-capped mountains. You start to row the boat towards the centre of the loch and, with each stroke of the oars, you go deeper and deeper into the picture. The oars hit the water again and again and you count the strokes: 1 - 2 - 3 - 4 - 5 - 6 - 7 - 8 - 9 - 10. You've now reached the centre and you stop to take a breather. You have a minute of clock time, equal to all the time you need, to appreciate the atmosphere and scenery of this extra special place

Just then your thoughts are interrupted as you notice a disturbance in the water near the boat. Ripples are spreading outwards as something large and grey starts to rise up from the depths and break through the surface. A head appears, but like no head you've ever seen before. The face turns and looks at you. You have a minute of clock time, equal to all the time you need, to take in what you can see.

The Loch Ness Monster now starts talking to you in a language you're familiar with and you listen carefully to what she has to say. You have a minute of clock time, equal to all the time you need, to listen to the personal message she has just for you and the message she has for mankind in general.

The time has come for Nessie to return to her underwater world and for you to make your journey home again, back to the place you started from. And with each stroke of the oars you feel more awake and ready for the life that lies ahead of you. Once again you start counting the strokes: 1 - 2- 3 - 4 - 5 - 6 - 7- 8 - 9 - 10. Welcome back!

Open your eyes now and stretch your arms and legs. Take a few minutes in silence to make some notes on the experi-ences you had on your journey, which you can then share with the rest of the group.

A Guided Visualisation: Avalon

Script for the guide (*to be read in a gentle, trance-inducing voice*)

Make yourself comfortable and close your eyes. Take a few deep breaths to help you relax. Feel the tension disappear stage by stage from the top of your head to the tips of your toes. Let your surroundings fade away as you gradually sink backwards through time and actuality and pass through the gateway of reality into the dreamtime. (*When the participants are fully relaxed, begin the next stage.*)

A thick, swirling fog surrounds you and as it gradually starts to clear you find yourself standing by the shore of a lake. Smell the long wet grass and feel the cold penetrating dampness in the air. Why have you been called to this place, you wonder. Morgan le Fey holds the answer to your question and you find the enchantress seated in a small fishing boat, waiting specially for you, to take you to the mystical isle of Avalon – the Celtic paradise.

Morgan le Fey's magical powers and beauty are legendary and you're totally magnetised by her. When you look into her eyes you get the feeling she can read your thoughts and that she knows you better than you know yourself. But at the same time you feel safe with her because her intentions are good and you sense that she means you no harm. You have a minute of clock time, equal to all the time you need, to appreciate the enchantress now gracing you with her presence. Morgan le Fey invites you to step into the boat and take the seat facing her. She smiles reassuringly at you, picks up the two wooden oars and starts to row. And with each stroke of the oars through the water, you find yourself going deeper and deeper into the dreamtime, deeper and deeper into a state of total surrender and relaxation.

Once the shore of the isle is in sight, Morgan le Fey lets go of the oars and the current gently carries the boat onto the sand. She steps out of the boat and motions to you to follow and you do so without hesitation as you know you can trust her with your very life.

She leads you up a flight of steps carved into the cliff. Higher and higher you climb until you reach the top. There you can see the whole island laid out before you like a banquet of exotic delicacies on a table. You have a minute of clock time, equal to all the time you need, to take in the landscape around you.

And now Morgan le Fey takes you to a rock pool filled with icy cold water. Somehow you already know what to do before she even asks. You strip off and immerse yourself. The shock of the cold water hits you and makes you gasp but Morgan urges you to stay with it and gradually you become acclimatised. You soak in its healing and restorative powers as it washes away all your troubles and cares. You have a minute of clock time, equal to all the time you need, to let the water purify and refresh.

❖
❖
❖
❖
❖
❖
❖
❖
❖
❖
❖
❖
❖
❖
❖

> The time has nearly come for your journey home but before I take you back, you're invited to choose a gift to take with you, a quality you lack that will help you, in your future life. You have a minute of clock time, equal to all the time you need, to select the gift that's appropriate for you.
>
> Morgan le Fey now leads you back down the cliff to the rowing boat on the beach. And with each stroke of the oars through the water, you draw away from the island and move closer to home as you return from the dreamtime through time to actuality, back, back, the same way you came, back to the place you started from. Welcome home!
>
> Open your eyes now and stretch your arms and legs. Take a few minutes in silence to make some notes on the experiences you had on your journey, which you can then share with the rest of the group.

Trying to conceptualise the use of different tenses in a foreign language can be frustrating for the language learner as it is only possible to apply the different forms once the concept has been internalised. Every language has some way to express time and in English time is often thought of as a "line". For example, you probably learnt history out of a book that had diagrams of events occurring in a line across a page. An example of a timeline for the Present Perfect is presented below. One way of helping students internalise the concept is to divide the room into two areas - past and present - with a line down the middle. Invite everyone to stand with you in the past and accompany you into the present sector on foot. "You've just walked from the present into the past" is then a perfect illustration of the target structure. This will also appeal to the kinesthetic intelligence type as it will give these learners a chance to stretch their legs! Timelines can be presented to students to illustrate the use of tenses or they can be invited to devise their own. Steve and Connirae Andreas in *Change Your Mind And Keep The Change* (1987) say that for most people "the past is usually a line off to the left, the present right in front of you, and the future in a line to the right." However, it has been found in NLP that each individual has his own way of sorting and organising time so it is probably preferable to allow the students to devise their own timelines instead of imposing your own model on them.

```
_____
      |                |               |
    Past            Present          Future
        ~~~~~~~~~~~~~~~~~~~~~~~~~~~~~~~~~>
```

Tony Buzan's *Mind Map* technique links left and right brain and encourages the learner to discern patterns and relationships. It is a non-linear form of note taking which links key words and ideas. In its simplest form, it could consist of the subject under discussion written in words inside a circle in the centre of the board, with arrows radiating from the circumference pointing to key vocabulary. An alternative would be to stick up a picture of the subject in the centre of the board. An example of a mind map is presented below to record new vocabulary on the topic of *Relationships*:

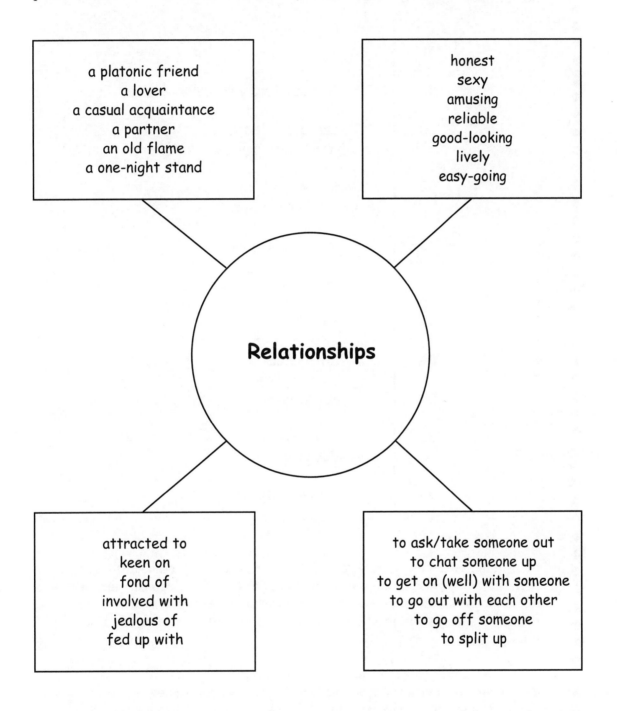

Lifelines can be used to provide an enjoyable and personal way of practising the Past Simple. Invite the students to draw a line and mark against it the key events in their lives, as in the example below. The lifelines can be drawn and illustrated to go on the classroom notice boards. The notes can be used for an exchange of information in class or as the starting point for a short written autobiography which could be completed for homework:

Year	Event
'51	born
'56	started primary school
'60	secondary school - hated every minute!
'65	first kiss - on holiday in Spain
'73	first teaching job
'78	first book published
'81	Brazil
'84	father died
'85	job in Spain
'91	a new flat in London
'96	married Ketevan

In a similar way, family trees can be drawn and can be used as a starting point for asking and talking about family relationships. Gaps can also be left in the family trees. The learners then exchange family trees with their neighbours, and they question each other to fill in the missing information.

Memory-mapping is a non-hierarchical, non-sequential method of making a summary or revision notes and can be used for the review stage of a lesson. The memory map can either be provided by the teacher or created by the students individually in a personalised way. You might like to make a memory map to summarise the contents of this Unit!

The ability to follow a map is indicative of spatial intelligence and the following activity provides an opportunity for the students to make use of this skill. **Faraway Places** practises the use of fixed expressions with the zero and definite articles and is suitable for students of Elementary level and above. After providing an example of your own to elicit the rules, invite the learners to work in pairs or small groups to complete the following account. (If geographical knowledge proves to be a problem, they can invent the names of the places or make use of maps.)

> Last year I/we sailed to ... **(a continent)** across the ... **(an ocean)** on the ... **(the name of a ship).**
>
> While I was/we were there I/we crossed the ... **(the name of a river)** and went on a tour to the ... **(a range of mountains)** because I/we wanted to climb Mount ... **(the name of a single mountain).**
>
> I/we then visited ... **(the name of a city)** where I/we stayed at the ... **(the name of a hotel).** I/we spent the afternoon in the ... **(the name of a gallery or a museum)** and in the evening I/we went to the ... **(the name of a concert hall or a theatre).**

When native speakers watch videos, they are criticised for being couch potatoes. However, watching TV or going to the cinema for the first time in a foreign language can be a daunting experience, and the use of short extracts of authentic material can help to build up the learners' confidence so they can then go on to tackle the real thing. The use of videos can be particularly effective to cater for spatial intelligence and there are three basic ways of using them in class:

- ◆ Silent viewing can be used to focus on the visual information, followed by groupwork to predict the nature of the dialogue.

- ◆ Sound only is also a possibility, with the students sitting with their backs to the screen, to stimulate discussion on what they think they will see and the use of the language of description.

- ◆ Then there is jigsaw viewing, in which the class is divided into two groups, one for silent viewing and the other for a sound only presentation. Students in group A then pair with students in group B to piece together the whole.

There are plenty of books available on how to use video in class but here is a suggestion for using TV advertising that you probably have not come across before. The same analysis form can be used for any commercial you show and it is presented below. Play the commercial, invite the students to complete the forms individually, then to compare their answers with their neighbours. An example of an analysed commercial and an explanation of some of the terminology could be presented to the class first before inviting them to complete their own forms.

TV Advertising Analysis Form

Selling:

....
....

Slogan:

....
....

Characters:

....
....
....
....

Storyline:

....
....
....
....
....
....
....
....
....
....

Soundtrack:

....
....

Possible Influences:

....
....

Idea:

....
....
....

Leaves you wondering:

....
....
....

Bottom line:

....
....

Our own strengths and weaknesses are, not surprisingly, reflected in our teaching styles. This is why it is so important for us as teachers to be aware of our own intelligence profiles so we can make adaptations in class to ensure we reach everyone in the group. I hope as you read through this book, my own weaknesses will not be apparent to you!

Unit 8: How To Cater For Intrapersonal Intelligence

A number of the activities presented in this book are multi-purpose in that they cater for more than one of the intelligence types. This also applies to relaxation techniques. As well as catering for bodily-kinesthetic intelligence, they also involve looking within. Intrapersonal intelligence indicates the ability to look within for causes and to find solutions to problems.

There are many different ways of relaxing and we each have a way that suits us best. Suggestions will only take root in the subconscious when the mind and body are sufficiently relaxed, so the more time we spend on facilitating this state before the start of a lesson or particular activity, the more successful the outcome is likely to be. Moreover, the current demand for stress-management books and courses confirms that knowing how to relax is one of the most useful skills we can learn.

The following exercise is adapted from a suggestion in *The Magical Classroom* by F. Noah Gordon (1995). If it is practical, ask the students to lie on the floor. They can make pillows to rest their heads on by rolling up a jacket or a pullover. (Words you might like to pre-teach before the exercise: fists / tight / muscles / tense / limp / shrug / stretch / yawn / wrinkle / stiff / sink / curl up.)

Script for the guide: Move around a bit until you get as comfortable as you can. Now close your eyes and think of your hands ... . Make tight fists with your hands ... as tight as you can. (*Pause several seconds.*) Good. Now relax your hands ... and feel the warm tingling sensation you get as your muscles say: "Ahh, we can relax now." Now bend your arms and make a muscle, making your arms very tense and tight. (*Pause several seconds.*) Now relax and let your arms go limp. Good. Now shrug your shoulders ... raising them up to your ears ... and hold them there for a few seconds, tightly. Okay, now let them go and notice how good that feels.

Still keeping your eyes closed, open your mouth wide, until you can feel your face muscles stretch ... like in an enormous yawn ... and close your mouth ... . Now press your tongue up against the roof of your mouth ... and really feel the pressure. Good. Now let it go and notice how good it feels to relax your tongue again. Okay, now wrinkle up your nose, make a funny face and hold it. (*Pause several seconds.*) Now let it go, and feel your face becoming very smooth and soft.

Now tighten your stomach muscles. (*Pause several seconds.*) Now relax them again ... just let them become soft and easy. Now tense all the muscles of your legs ... as stiffly as you can ... and hold the position. (*Pause several seconds.*) Good. Now relax your legs ... and notice how warm and good they feel, almost like sinking into the floor ... Now curl up your toes really tight ... hold them in that position ... then relax.

Now ... take three slow, deep breaths, and each time blow the air out so you can hear yourself exhale. Breathe in the warm light, and breathe out all of your tightness ... . Breathe in the warm light and breathe out all of your tightness ... . Breathe in the warm light and breathe out all of your tightness ... . Now open your eyes and smile at someone!

Two further relaxation techniques are presented below, taken from *Accelerated Learning in the Classroom* by Alistair Smith (1996):

> "Firstly, close your eyes and then, one stage at a time, relax each part of your body. Breathe evenly and gently. As you progress, repeat to yourself in a progressively slower monotone: now I relax my eyes ... now I relax my mouth ... now I relax my neck ... now I relax my shoulders ... now I relax my arms ... now I relax my chest ... now I relax my stomach ... now I relax my legs ... now I relax my feet.
>
> Sit or stand in an upright position. Place your clasped hands on your stomach. Breathe evenly and gently. Breathe from your belly first, filling up your stomach and chest like a balloon. Continue to breathe as your chest rises. Continue to breathe into your throat. Then gently exhale. Repeat the exercise. It may help to visualise the air filling up like a balloon as you go."

Autogenic training, mandala, transcendental meditation, or yoga for relaxation can all be used for the purpose of creating an atmosphere conducive to learning. In fact, the list of possibilities is endless. The technique below is known as "The Breath on the Left" and it has also been found to be effective.

> Sit still in a chair with your spine straight, eyes closed and with your left hand relaxed in your lap. Bring the right hand up and block off the right nostril with your right thumb. Begin long, deep breathing through the left nostril. Relax the abdomen to bring the air into the lower lungs, then expand the chest. Continue the long deep breathing a minimum of twelve times. Then inhale, hold for five seconds, exhale and relax.
>
> Then reverse the process, blocking the left nostril and breathing through the right.

Alternate breathing can help to unite the two brain hemispheres and make learners feel more relaxed and centred. The following exercise adapted from *Relaxation* by Nitya Lacroix (1995) can be used for this purpose.

> 1. Sit in a comfortable position with your eyes closed and try to keep your spine straight. With the first two fingers of your right hand tucked into the palm, use the right thumb to close the right nostril. The breath can be deep and can go into the chest, head and back, but there should be no strain.
>
> 2. When you want to exhale, release the right nostril and block the left (with the third finger of the left hand). The exhaled breath flows out of the right side. Now breathe in through the same nostril and change fingers to breathe out through the other side.

If you are working with adult learners, it is more than likely they will have some relaxation techniques of their own and they can lead the class through the exercises instead of you taking centre stage. There can be no greater boost to their confidence than having such opportunities, and we should create them whenever we can.

♦ Learner diaries can be useful, particularly as an alternative to conventional forms of homework. The students are encouraged to keep an ongoing journal throughout the course, which becomes a written exchange of ideas based upon the experiences and reflections of reader and writer. They give you an opportunity to show you value the learners' ideas and are not just interested in correcting their mistakes. Moreover, they give the students an opportunity to bring up personal concerns they might not feel comfortable about raising in class – their lack of confidence or their frustration at their lack of progress, for example. Another possibility along similar lines is to write every member of class an individual letter on day one of the course, introducing yourself and inviting a reply. To the students who respond to this initiative, you can then correspond on a regular basis. Although this involves a lot of extra work on your part, the results can be both revealing and rewarding. The feedback you obtain can help you adapt the course content to cater more for the learners' individual needs and interests.

♦ Incorporating MI Theory into teaching promotes individualised instruction. In other words, the learning process is adapted to the particular students – taking their learning styles and intelligence types into account when planning your lessons. This should not be confused with self-instruction, which refers to situations in which a learner is working without the direct control of the teacher.

♦ Self-instruction can either be learner-centred or materials-centred. With the former, the teacher seeks to include the learners increasingly in the decision-making process about their learning and the management of it. With the latter, the materials are designed in such a way that the decision making and management of the learning are built in. Both cater for the intrapersonal intelligence type. Learner contracts can help towards facilitating this process as they provide learners with a framework for their planning and a brief check list of things they have to take into account. The minimal contract will suggest to the learner that he decided what work he is going to do over what period and this can be devised in consultation with the teacher. Learner contracts involve goal-setting and the students can have an opportunity to review their progress and adapt their programmes during a weekly "round" or feedback session. The advantages of self-instruction include the fact that it can be seen as a process of empowerment. Most of the significant language learning which people undertake at different stages of their lives occurs outside the classroom and unassisted by a teacher. Promoting learner autonomy helps to equip students to do this both efficiently and effectively.

♦ Project work provides learners with an opportunity to be more autonomous. This could entail the students preparing a presentation to give to the class about the city or country they come from or perhaps their hobbies. At higher levels it could even entail researching and then presenting a grammar point to the rest of the class.

◆ Creative writing, especially poetry, involves looking within and appeals to the intrapersonal intelligence type. A *haiku* is a Japanese poem that consists of three lines - with five syllable, seven syllables and five syllables. When you have a class of students 'who think they know everything', you might like to set them the following task to work on individually. Invite them to produce *haiku* on a particular topic with one line containing the zero article, one line with the indefinite article and one line with the definite article!

Three examples are presented below:

True love is a myth
For it has no existence
Except in the mind

Friendship is precious
Like raindrops caught in the hand
Of a dying man

A true friend like you
I would search the world to find
Soulfood and lifeblood

◆ Writing poetry can be done individually or collectively. After reading the following Adrian Henri poem to the class, you can invite everyone to write one line expressing their own interpretation of what love is. Alternatively, the students can work in groups of three to produce a four-line verse in the same form as the original. The results can be collated and displayed on the notice boards. The title **Love Is...** could be changed to **Happiness Is...** or anything else that suits your purpose.

Love Is...

Love is feeling cold in the back of vans
Love is a fanclub with only two fans
Love is walking holding painstained hands
Love is ...

Love is fish and chips on winter nights
Love is blankets full of strange delights
Love is when you don't put out the lights
Love is ...

Love is presents in Christmas shops
Love is when you're feeling Top of the Pops
Love is what happens when the music stops
Love is ...

Love is white panties lying all forlorn
Love is a pink nightdress still slightly warm
Love is when you have to leave at dawn
Love is ...

Love is you and love is me
Love is a prison and love is free
Love's what's there when you're away from me
Love is...

(published in *The Mersey Sound*, 1967)

◆ Inviting the students to write postcards can produce interesting results too. Collect all the postcards you receive from friends, stick a blank piece of white paper over the writing and you will soon build up a varied collection of views. Invite each member of the class to select a view that appeals to them, then ask them to imagine they are on holiday at the place shown and to write a postcard to someone else in the class describing their experiences. You can then play the part of postman and deliver the cards to the addressees. You can also use the opportunity to explore the language of postcard writing - *Having a fantastic time* rather than *I am having a fantastic time*, for example.

◆ By incorporating a review stage into your lesson plan, you provide the students with opportunity to reflect on what they have learnt. This could take the form of a guided visualisation and a sample script for this purpose is presented in the final chapter of this book. Alternatively, the learners can be provided with or invited to create a mnemonic device to help them to remember what they have studied. I can remember what happened to the wives of King Henry VIII this way - divorced, beheaded, died, divorced, beheaded, survived!

The following games cater for both interpersonal and intrapersonal intelligences for, as well as incorporating pairwork, they also involve the students' looking within to find the required information.

The Indefinite Article Game *is an activity for Advanced level learners in which the students have thirty seconds to talk about something that belongs to them without using the definite article. The secret lies in constantly introducing new information and in not referring to it more than once. Another trick is to use the classifying function of the indefinite article. (The classifying uses of the indefinite article are underlined in the example presented below and the function in each case is to assign a person, animal or thing to a special class or kind.) The game can be played in pairs, with the person not talking holding a gong or a whistle which can be sounded whenever the forbidden word is used.*

I've got a cat called Micia - an Italian name. She's a stray black cat and about five years old. Her favourite toy is a mouse she likes to play with and she also has a small rubber ball with a bell in it. In winter she sleeps in my bedroom in a basket but in summer she often stays out all night on an adventure and I don't know where she goes. When she returns she sometimes brings me a dead bird as a present, which she deposits on my bed for my breakfast!

A cat can be a good companion to have when you live on your own and research suggests that having a pet at home can reduce your chances of getting a serious illness. Another advantage of having a cat rather than a child is that it's more independent and costs a lot less to feed and clothe. Having a cat is an interesting challenge as you have to win its love whereas a dog will always love you however you behave. As far as I'm concerned, no home is complete without a cat and Micia is my very best friend.

The Just-A-Minute Game is an activity for Advanced level learners. The students have sixty seconds to talk about their favourite hobby using as many examples of the gerund as they can within the time limit. The learners can work in pairs on the activity and take it in turns to play the game. The listener is responsible for watching the clock and for counting the number of times the gerund is used. Alternatively, the talks can be recorded and played back for everyone to hear. An example of sixty seconds on my favourite hobby is presented below.

Although there are good reasons to be frightened of **gambling** because of the risk of **losing** so much and of **becoming** addicted to the habit, I have to admit that I find it irresistible. I'm particularly interested in **betting** on horses and I'm in the habit of **having** a flutter every Saturday afternoon, then **watching** the races on TV. I know that some people prefer **going** to casinos to feed their habits but I don't like **having** to dress up in a suit and tie and the added attraction of **horseracing** is that you lose your money more slowly! I also enjoy **playing** the National Lottery and look forward to **watching** the draw on TV every Saturday evening – the highlight of my week. My wife says I'm in danger of **becoming** a couch potato because I spend so much time **sitting** in front of the box **eating** junk food. She's much more active than I am and prefers **playing** tennis or **going** to our local Health Club. She's intent on **persuading** me to join her but I'm perfectly happy the way I am and can see no reason for **changing** my ways. I appreciate **having** the opportunity of **spending** some time on my own and I find it an enjoyable way of **relaxing** and **turning** off from my work. Some people dream of **giving** up their jobs and **travelling** around the world if they have a big win but I'd enjoy **having** my own private swimming pool – something I've always wanted ever since I was a child.

To conclude this unit, here is a lesson plan for a storytelling session which invites the learners to look within. The story is presented on the following pages, followed by the plan.

Who Am I?

A poor man who had spent all his life in forests resolved to try his fortune in a great city, and as he drew near it he observed with wonder the crowds on the road. He thought "I shall certainly not be able to know myself among so many people if I have not something about me that the others have not." So he tied a pumpkin to his right leg and, thus decorated, entered the town.

A young wag, perceiving the simpleton, made friends with him, and induced him to spend the night at his house. While he was asleep, the joker removed the pumpkin from his leg and tied it to his own, and then lay down again.

In the morning, when the poor fellow awoke and found the pumpkin on his companion's leg, he called to him, "Hey! get up, for I am perplexed in my mind. Who am I, and who are you? If I am I, why is the pumpkin on your leg? And if you are you, why is the pumpkin not on my leg?"

1. *Explain or elicit what a pumpkin is, then invite the students to make a list of all the uses it could be put to. They can work on this in groups.*

2. *Narrate the story.*

3. *Pause after* "and induced him to spend the night at his house". *Ask the class to predict what follows:* What do you think the young wag did to the simpleton during the night?

4. *Invite the students to write the question* "Who am I?" *on a piece of paper. Tell them to put down their pens, pick them up with their other hands and to write the first answer that comes into their heads. Repeat the process with the questions* "Why am I here?" *and* "Where am I going?". *The answers can then be shared and discussed by the class as a whole.*

5. *An alternative way of finding answers to the questions above could be by completing the questionnaire presented on the following page.*

What Do You Want Out Of Life?

1. What kind of future would you like to be able to offer your children?
   a. a pollution-free environment
   b. a heritage rich in culture
   c. a free-thinking, permissive society

2. What do you like doing on a cold winter's evening?
   a. curling up in front of the fire with your partner
   b. engaging in a heated political discussion with friends
   c. going to a disco

3. How would you describe your friends?
   a. respectable and hardworking
   b. eccentric academics or artists
   c. fun-loving hedonists

4. What would you least like to be deprived of?
   a. your credit cards
   b. your books
   c. your passport

5. What would your ideal holiday be?
   a. in a luxury hotel by the seaside
   b. on an island with archeological sites to visit
   c. trekking through the Amazon jungle

6. What would you buy a friend for their birthday?
   a. something useful for the home
   b. an interesting book
   c. something unusual and exotic

7. How would you define your main goal in life?
   a. to have a successful marriage
   b. to expand your mind to its maximum potential
   c. to live every second to the full

8. How would you prefer to spend the day?
   a. by following the same pattern you normally do
   b. having the opportunity to learn something new
   c. having it filled with stimulating experiences

9. What's your favourite smell?
   a. freshly baked bread
   b. musty old buildings
   c. incense

10. How would you like to be described?
    a. as a kind and caring person
    b. as being bright and full of ideas
    c. as a bit of a character

What Your Score Means

If you've scored mostly "a"s, your main need is for security. You have a liking for things that are familiar rather than novel, safe rather than exciting, and stable rather than changeable. Perhaps you're missing out on some of the colour and thrills of life.

If you've scored mostly "b"s, you're the sort of person who would be happy living in a big city as your main need is for intellectual and cultural stimulation. You're interesting company to be with but possibly lacking in warmth.

If you've scored mostly "c"s, you're a fun-loving person, adventurous and determined to enjoy life to the full. You probably have lots of friends but your critics might accuse you of being shallow and unreliable.

Unit 9: How To Cater For Naturalist Intelligence

Naturalist intelligence is the ability to recognise plants, animals, and other parts of the natural environment such as clouds or rocks. This ability can also be used to deal with the world of man-made objects. When students look for patterns in the world around them, they see order instead of chaos, which builds confidence in their understanding of how the world (or a language) works and gives them greater control over it. As Jacob Bronowski says, "A man becomes creative ... when he finds a new unity in the variety of nature. He does so by finding a likeness between things which were not thought alike before, and this gives him a sense of richness and of understanding." (From "Patterns And The Eighth Intelligence", *Mindshift Connection*, Zephyr Press.) Culture itself can be defined as the way we order, classify, and organise the world around us through language. It would seem that this eighth intelligence not only has its own identity but is also used to enrich the other seven as each of the original seven intelligences draws upon patterning skills to interpret the sights and the sounds of the world around us.

Naturalist intelligence can be catered for in the ELT classroom by noticing relationships, categorising and classifying. Observing plants and animals or collecting rocks would not appear to be immediately relevant and neither would listening to the sounds created in the natural world. However, the natural sounds could be used in the background to help create an atmosphere conducive to the students' feeling relaxed and able to produce their best work

Two topic-based categorising activities are presented on the following pages to practise the use of the tenses, dealing with how couples first met each other. The first contrasts the use of the Past Simple with the Past Continuous and the second includes a whole range of tenses.

How We Met

Separate the sentences into two stories. There are seven parts in one and eight in the other. Label each part "a" or "b" as in the examples:

a. We were both students at University College London.

b. We first met each other at a party – in the bathroom to be exact.

a. He was a second year geology student and I'd just come back from a year in France to start my final year in the French department.

___ Our memories of our first meeting differ. He thinks he first saw me sitting at an open window smoking Gauloises.

___ It was really embarrassing because he'd forgotten to lock the door and I walked in to find him doing up his trousers.

___ In fact, we'd met a few days earlier. I noticed him one morning when I was jogging through Hyde Park.

___ It was a fancy dress party and I was dressed as a belly dancer.

___ Anyway, after I'd apologised he introduced himself and we started chatting to each other.

___ Our first date was in October, on the night the clocks went back.

___ Then we heard someone banging on the door.

___ "Who's in there? It's been occupied for ages!"

___ We made the most of the extra hour by going to a late night film.

___ Too embarrassed to walk out together, we decided to climb out of the window and re-entered through the front door when nobody was looking.

___ I think it was "The Titanic".

___ Although we've had our ups and downs since the party, surprisingly we're still together.

How We Met

Separate the sentences into two stories. There are eight parts in one and nine in the other. Label each part "a" or "b" as in the examples:

a. My sister had just found a room to rent in a house with three other people.

b. I met my girlfriend when I was working as a teacher.

b. She came to the school to improve her English.

___ When I returned home late from a weekend in Manchester, she put me up for the night.

___ She's a bilingual secretary and she comes from Brazil.

___ The house is in the suburbs of London where she's a medical student.

___ At first she didn't seem to be very interested in me.

___ After she'd been in the school for a couple of weeks, I finally plucked up enough courage to invite her to a party.

___ It was so uncomfortable sleeping on the floor that as soon as my sister got up to go to work, I immediately jumped into her bed and went back to sleep.

___ Suddenly there was a knock on the door and one of her flatmates walked in.

___ We soon discovered we had a lot in common and we've been going out together ever since.

___ He'd woken me up so I agreed to have a coffee with him downstairs.

___ We ended up spending the whole day together.

___ At the moment she's studying for the Cambridge First Certificate exam.

___ Although we've been happily married for some time now, I'm the one who always makes the coffee.

___ Fortunately she isn't in my class and we've managed to avoid any embarrassment.

___ My husband's been a GP since he left medical college but he's studying to become a specialist.

Now look at the following account of how two people met and change the verbs into the correct tenses:

A couple of years ago I **1. (go)** to Switzerland on holiday. It **2. (be)** the first time I **3. (ever go)** skiing and I **4. (look)** forward to it. However, the first day on the skiing slope I **5. (break)** my leg and **6. (end)** up in hospital. As you can imagine, I **7. (feel)** really depressed until I **8. (meet)** the nurse who **9. (be)** later to become my wife! The moment she **10. (enter)** the hospital ward it **11. (be)** love at first sight. At the moment we **12. (live)** with my parents but we **13. (both work)** hard to save up enough money to buy a home of our own. We **14. (be)** married for just over a year and for our first wedding anniversary my wife **15. (buy)** me a pair of skis!

Write a short account, true or imaginary, of how you and your partner first met. Use as many different tenses as you can.

Answers

1. went
2. was
3. I'd ever gone
4. I'd been looking
5. broke
6. ended
7. was feeling
8. met
9. was
10. entered
11. was
12. we're living
13. we're both working
14. we've been
15. bought

The four activities presented below were produced for an Elementary level class. The words could be enlarged, printed on card and then cut up for the learners to arrange in suitable groups.

Word Groups (1)

Make five groups of five words, and give each group a name:

leg
a lesson
uncle   Example: **school**   - a lesson
a garden   - a student
red   - a homework
                                                 - a teacher
daughter   - a classroom
homework
grandfather
shoulder
yellow

green
elbow
a park
cousin
grass

a student
blue
parents
arm
a teacher

a tree
foot
a classroom
white
a flower

Answers

school
colours
relations
parts of the body
plants

Word Groups (2)

Make five groups of five words, and give each group a name:

a cow
a chair
paper
a plane
a pen

a pilot
a sofa
an elephant
a pencil
a teacher

a ship
a cupboard
an eraser
a monkey
a bus

a dog
a sharpener
a car
a bookcase
a nurse

a table
a typist
a train
a dentist
a giraffe

Answers

animals
furniture
stationery
forms of transport
professions

Word Groups (3)

Make five groups of five words, and give each group a name:

a cup
tomatoes
hair
bananas
a shirt

a skirt
a mouth
an onion
a nose
a spoon

peas
boots
an apple
eyes
grapes

a jacket
a plate
ears
a knife
a potato

a fork
a melon
trousers
a carrot
a pear

Answers

tableware
vegetables
parts of the head
fruit
clothes

WORD GROUPS 4

Make five groups of five words, and give each group a name:

tea
a trumpet
golf
a writer
beer

tennis
a lion
a guitar
a horse
football

a soldier
a flute
coffee
a drum
a sailor

a rabbit
milk
basketball
wine
a cello

a bear
an actor
swimming
an engineer
a mouse

Answers

animals
drinks
musical instruments
sports
professions

The word groups presented below could be used on Advanced level classes. Invite the students to divide each set of twenty five words into groups of five according to topics, then to suggest a title for each group:

Group A

a minor	a divorcee	lobster	a spinster	cod
sole	plaice	Satan	thigh	halo
a widower	a widow	lap	an adolescent	paradise
soul	hell	prawn	calf	a bachelor
a youth	a juvenile	a teenager	shin	knee

Group B

sage	cheeks	rosemary	anchor	nostrils
hull	parsley	mast	chin	pepper
a beetroot	temple	a tomato	a radish	celery
brow	ginger	mint	thyme	rudder
cloves	deck	cinnamon	lettuce	nutmeg

Group C

a wing	dawn	a jet	plump	frost
dyed	straight	grey	claws	skinny
a nest	an egg	daybreak	a parachute	a seatbelt
obese	shapely	slim	feathers	curly
a cockpit	dew	a beak	permed	sunrise

Group D

a plane	a bough	a spanner	a coffin	a branch
a twig	a morgue	a necklace	a hammer	a grave
an earring	a stethoscope	an undertaker	a scalpel	a bracelet
a corpse	a pendant	a chisel	a log	a screwdriver
a barometer	a trunk	a thermometer	a brooch	a microscope

Group E

a cot	a yacht	a bunk	a witness	a tanker
a tug	a bride	a groom	a cradle	a hammock
confetti	a gypsy	an astrologer	a prophet	a shoal
a palmist	a barge	a liner	a swarm	a honeymoon
a herd	a flock	a pack	a put-you-up	a clairvoyant

Group F

chess	a potter	a nightcap	a silversmith	darts
a nightmare	a nap	an acrobat	an insomniac	a juggler
an arsonist	an embezzler	a shoplifter	a pickpocket	draughts
a ringmaster	a clown	bingo	a somnambulist	a blackmailer
dominoes	a weaver	a carpenter	a blacksmith	an escapologist

Answers

Group A

minor/teenager/youth/adolescent/juvenile
widower/spinster/bachelor/widow/divorcee
Satan/hell/paradise/soul/ halo
knee/thigh/shin/lap/calf
sole/plaice/cod/prawn/lobster

Group B

sage/parsley/thyme/rosemary/mint
beetroot/celery/radish/tomato/lettuce
ginger/nutmeg/cloves/pepper/cinnamon
mast/anchor/deck/rudder/hull
brow/temple/chin/nostrils/cheeks

Group C

straight/permed/curly/grey/dyed
slim/obese/skinny/plump/shapely
seatbelt/jet/parachute/wing/cockpit
nest/claws/feathers/egg/beak
dew/sunrise/dawn/frost/daybreak

Group D

log/twig/bough/trunk/branch
hammer/chisel/plane/screwdriver/spanner
bracelet/necklace/brooch/pendant/earring
morgue/grave/undertaker/coffin/corpse
barometer/stethoscope/scalpel/thermometer/microscope

Group E

hammock/bunk/cradle/cot/put-you-up
palmist/astrologer/gypsy/clairvoyant/prophet
witness/bride/honeymoon/groom/confetti
tug/liner/barge/tanker/yacht
herd/swarm/flock/shoal/pack

Group F

darts/chess/dominoes/bingo/draughts
escapologist/acrobat/clown/ringmaster/juggler
nightmare/insomniac/nap/somnambulist/nightcap
potter/silversmith/weaver/carpenter/blacksmith
shoplifter/embezzler/pickpocket/arsonist/blackmailer

In order to live in the world, we must name it. Names are essential for the construction of reality for without a name it is difficult to accept the existence of an object, an event, a feeling. Vocabulary is essential for categorising or classifying, which is why it is so important. Moreover, words are not used in isolation. As Michael Lewis (head of Language Teaching Publications, and the developer of the Lexical approach) points out, they appear in chunks of language, which is why work on collocations is so useful to help facilitate the production of new language.

Whenever new vocabulary is introduced, the students can be invited to suggest useful collocates and to record them in the form of a table as in the example below. Alternatively, they can be encouraged to make use of a dictionary designed for this purpose – the *Language Teaching Publications Dictionary of Selected Collocations*, for example.

to sleep

- soundly
- restlessly
- peacefully
- intermittently
- fitfully

to see a(n)

- attend
- miss
- give
- sit through

- outstanding
- average
- disappointing
- brilliant

performance

to react

- positively
- calmly
- violently
- negatively
- favourably

The activities presented on the following pages are designed for Advanced level students and deal with collocations that form idioms.

Match the numbers on the left with the letters on the right. Then use each of the collocations once to complete the sentences:

1. cool		a.	fiddle
2. dead-end		b.	gloves
3. golden		c.	hand
4. flying		d.	head
5. hot		e.	job
6. kid		f.	opportunity
7. old		g.	partner
8. open		h.	potato
9. plain		i.	sailing
10. second		j.	secret
11. sleeping		k.	talk
12. small		l.	visit

1. When she found out that he was married, she dropped him like a ... .
2. It helps to have a ... on your shoulders in this job and not to be too impulsive.
3. He's full of self-importance and not prepared to play ... to anyone.
4. If you feel you're stuck in a ... , then why don't you take control of your life and do something about it?
5. Although they do their best to paper over the cracks, the fact that their marriage is on the rocks is an ... .
6. I know it hasn't been easy for you but hopefully it will be ... from now on.
7. He's highly sensitive by nature so you'd better handle him with ... .
8. I can see that you know what you're doing and you're clearly an ... at the game.
9. Although she invested a lot of money in the company, she doesn't take an active role – she's just a ... .
10. It's a. ... so make the most of it!
11. Let's cut out the ... and get straight down to business.
12. I'm afraid I won't be able to stay very long – it's just a ... .

Answers

1-d		1.	hot potato
2-e		2.	cool head
3-f		3.	second fiddle
4-l		4.	dead-end job
5-h		5.	open secret
6-b		6.	plain sailing
7-c		7.	kid gloves
8-j		8.	old hand
9-i		9.	sleeping partner
10-a		10.	golden opportunity
11-g		11.	small talk
12-k		12.	flying visit

Match the numbers on the left with the letters on the right. Then use each of the collocations once to complete the sentences:

1. dark		a. certainty
2. dead		b. drugs
3. dirty		c. horse
4. easy		d. line
5. hard		e. one
6. high		f. option
7. last		g. spirits
8. number		h. supply
9. package		i. times
10. party		j. tour
11. short		k. word
12. soft		l. work

1. Why do you always give me the ... to do? Why don't you give it to someone else for a change?
2. She's a very stubborn person and always insists on having the ... .
3. The MP was criticised by the Prime Minister for not toeing the ... .
4. Good jobs are in ... these days so you'll just have to take what you can get.
5. How do you feel about the use of ... ?
6. The only reason why I applied for the job was that I thought it would be an ... .
7. You're a ... , aren't you? I had no idea you'd turn out to be such a star.
8. The favourite's bound to win the big race – it's a ... .
9. I know you've been through ... recently but you're tough and you'll weather the storm.
10. Don't worry about everyone else – think of ... and put yourself first.
11. You're in ... today, aren't you? It makes a welcome change from your usual miserable self!
12. I know you're independent by nature but how would you feel about going on a ... with me?

Answers

1-c	1. dirty work
2-a	2. last word
3-l	3. party line
4-f	4. short supply
5-i	5. soft drugs
6-g	6. easy option
7-k	7. dark horse
8-e	8. dead certainty
9-j	9. hard times
10-d	10. number one
11-h	11. high spirits
12-b	12. package tour

Match the numbers on the left with the letters on the right. Then use each of the collocations once to complete the sentences:

1. affect		a. amends
2. bury		b. corners
3. cross		c. a flutter
4. cut		d. forces
5. do		e. the hatchet
6. have		f. heart
7. join		g. your hopes
8. lose		h. ignorance
9. make		i. the light
10. raise		j. shop
11. see		k. swords
12. talk		l. the trick

1. When you mix business with pleasure, you end up ... all the time.
2. I know you're finding the course difficult but please don't ... because I'm sure you'll succeed in the end.
3. If we ... , nobody will be able to stand in our way.
4. I'd like to ... for all the trouble I've caused you by inviting you out for a meal.
5. Instead of trying to ... , just take your time and do the job properly.
6. I'm not a heavy gambler but I do like to ... on the horses now and then.
7. What happened in the past is all water under the bridge now so let's ... and make a fresh start.
8. I know how much you want the job but don't ... too high or you might be disappointed.
9. Don't ... with me or you'll live to regret it!
10. She might ... but don't be taken in because there's more to her than meets the eye.
11. If you feel you need to get away from it all, a weekend in the country should ... .
12. He didn't have a clue what to do at first but I think he's finally beginning to ... .

Answers

1-h	1. talking shop
2-e	2. lose heart
3-k	3. join forces
4-b	4. make amends
5-l	5. cut corners
6-c	6. have a flutter
7-d	7. bury the hatchet
8-f	8. raise your hopes
9-a	9. cross swords
10-g	10. affect ignorance
11-i	11. do the trick
12-j	12. see the light

Match the numbers on the left with the letters on the right. Then use each of the collocations once to complete the sentences:

1. at	a. my back
2. behind	b. the brain
3. between	c. common
4. by	d. a disadvantage
5. for	e. the full
6. in	f. heart
7. off	g. the lines
8. on	h. the peg
9. out of	i. reason
10. to	j. sorts
11. under	k. the sun
12. within	l. the world

1. As you've played the game before and I haven't, I'm ... .
2. They get on really well together because they have so much ... .
3. Hypochondriacs imagine they have every illness ... .
4. Did you buy the suit ... or did you have it made to measure?
5. If you ask me, he's got women ... – they're all he ever seems to talk about.
6. I didn't mean to hurt you – I wouldn't want to upset you ... .
7. She's the sort of person who believes in living life ... and throws herself enthusiastically into whatever she does.
8. It's no good lying to me – you've been seeing someone ... , haven't you?
9. I could never understand physics when I was at school so I just had to learn all the textbooks ... .
10. If you're feeling ... , you should take a day off work.
11. I'm not the monster you seem to think I am and I'm prepared to consider any request ... .
12. I know what's written in the brochure but you have to read ... to get an accurate picture.

Answers

1-d	1. at a disadvantage
2-a	2. in common
3-g	3. under the sun
4-f	4. off the peg
5-l	5. on the brain
6-c	6. for the world
7-h	7. to the full
8-b	8. behind my back
9-j	9. by heart
10-e	10. out of sorts
11-k	11. within reason
12-i	12. between the lines

Match the numbers on the left with the letters on the right. Then use each of the collocations once to complete the sentences:

1. curry		a. favour
2. gain		b. a fuss
3. go		c. ground
4. hit		d. halves
5. keep		e. my hand
6. kill		f. your head
7. know		g. your luck
8. lose		h. the roof
9. make		i. the score
10. push		j. stock
11. show		k. time
12. take		l. touch

1. I know how angry you must be feeling but try to ... and avoid losing your temper.
2. The Opposition has clearly been ... recently and the Government is under a great deal of pressure.
3. I hope we're not going to ... with each other and we'll always remain good friends.
4. It's only a cut, not a serious injury, and you're ... over nothing.
5. He's trying to ... with his boss but he doesn't seem to be getting very far.
6. You can entrust her with the job because she ... and you can be sure she won't let you down.
7. Be thankful for what you've already achieved and don't ... too far.
8. It's time you ... of your situation and gave some thought to your future.
9. If you turn up late for work again, your boss will ... !
10. There's no reason why you should have to foot the bill so I suggest that we ... .
11. If I were you, I wouldn't ... too soon – I'd try to keep a few tricks up my sleeve.
12. If you've got nothing to do, you could ... by giving me a hand!

Answers

1-a		1. keep your head
2-c		2. gaining ground
3-d		3. lose touch
4-h		4. making a fuss
5-f		5. curry favour
6-k		6. knows the score
7-i		7. push your luck
8-l		8. took stock
9-b		9. hit the roof
10-g		10. go halves
11-e		11. show my hand
12-j		12. kill time

The Collocation Game can be used to practise these connections and some samples for Intermediate level students are presented on the following pages. Here are the instructions:

Shuffle the cards and deal them equally, face down, among the four players. The players then take it in turns to lay down a card under one of the four headings on the board. If a card is placed in an inappropriate column, the other players can challenge it. If the challenge is correct, the player of the wrong card has to take an extra card from the challenger's hand as a penalty. The winner is the first player to succeed in laying down all his/her cards correctly.

Game One

To take	To have	To break	To catch

Cards For Game One

		+++ 171 +++	
a break	a headache	a leg	a cold
an exam	a haircut	a window	a bus
a seat	breakfast	the law	someone's attention
a taxi	a holiday	a world record	a ball
someone's temperature	a bath	someone's heart	a thief
a look	a relationship	a promise	a fright
a chance	a drink	the rules	a surprise
notes	time	a habit	fire
a rest	a rest	the ice	someone's eye
someone's place	a problem	the news to someone	a mouse

Game Two

To pay	To keep	To save	To find

Cards For Game Two

attention	a pet	time	a partner
the bill	control	money	time
interest	a promise	someone's life	the answer
the price	calm	energy	happiness
cash	a secret	one's strength	a way
by cheque	someone's place	someone a seat	the money
someone a visit	an appointment	oneself trouble	a solution
a salary	quiet	electricity	space
someone a compliment	a diary	space	a replacement
wages	the change	a penalty	a cure

A Multiple Intelligences Road To An ELT Classroom

Game Three

To get	To make	To miss	To do

Game Three

Cards For Game Three

home	progress	a goal	homework
frightened	an effort	a chance	the shopping
the sack	money	the point	the housework
permission	a mess	a flight	someone a favour
ready	trouble	an opportunity	the cooking
a surprise	a mistake	one's family	business
the message	furniture	a lesson	nothing
lost	a noise	one's home	the washing up
a job	peace	an appointment	a job
nowhere	a change	someone's help	one's best

Game Four

To go	To come	To get	To feel

Cards For Game Four

mad	first	ready	tense
wild	last	married	comfortable
crazy	right	started	happy
bad	second	lost	proud
white	early	divorced	free
abroad	close	burnt	nervous
missing	prepared	drunk	old
quiet	late	angry	disappointed
dark	direct	wet	hurt
overseas	complete	worried	sleepy

◆ Finding connections where none seem to exist could also prove to be productive. As an alternative to finding the odd man out, students could be invited to work in groups to find connections between apparently disparate items. Moreover, once they are familiar with the exercise type, they can be invited to produce their own groups to test each other.

Find the odd man out:

> boiled / fried / poached / roasted / scrambled

Answer: "roasted" because eggs are not normally cooked this way

Find the connection:

> a chair / a horse / a rabbit / a table / a tortoise

Answer: They can all have four legs!

◆ Another way of finding connections between apparently disparate items is by making use of metaphor – asking the students to find the same relationships between words as between different members of a family, for example. Find pairs of words which are *Husbands & Wives* – like "salt & pepper" or *Mother & Daughters* – like "moon & stars". This could take the form of a team game in which each team has a certain number of minutes to make as many such connections as they can from a list of words provided. To score points, they would need to be able to justify the pairings they make.

What about the connection between naturalist intelligence and nature? Not so easy when you work in a language school in Oxford Street in Central London! However, outdoor activities could well be a possibility along the following lines. Your students go out with a notebook and pen, preferably where there are other people, to take notes on their observations for a certain period of time. Prepare the students beforehand on what they should be observing: **What are the people wearing? What are they doing? Why do you think they are doing that?** etc. When they return they can write about what they saw. This could be used to provide practice in the use of the Past Continuous with Pre-Intermediate students – **I saw a man who was playing the guitar and singing a song/I saw an old woman who was feeding the pigeons** ..... etc.

Other possibilities could include having students describe an actual outdoor scene. This description can then be given to another pair who are to draw the scene based on the description - an information gap activity. You could invite someone to imagine that they are a natural object. They then have to answer questions about themselves until another member of the class guesses what they are – a variation on the popular **Twenty Questions** game.

Naturalist intelligence can also be applied to work on phonology. Working in small groups, the students can be invited to think of three words for each of two contrasting sounds – a verb, a noun and an adjective. If the sounds were /v/ and /b/, the words could be **violet / very / virtual** and **banana / beautiful / bus**. Then ask the learners to make sentences containing all six words and the result will be their very own tongue-twister. **A very beautiful violet got on the banana-coloured virtual bus,** for example.

Unit 10: The SAFER Teaching Model

First there was the PPP model, then there was ARC, and now there is OHE too. You are probably wondering what the next model will be. How about the SAFER teaching model? The five stages of the cycle are described below:

 Set the scene to create optimal learning conditions. This includes building a supportive learning environment by promoting the students' self-esteem and self-belief. The first stage of the Suggestopedic Cycle can be useful for this purpose.

Creating the right kind of atmosphere is crucial to the success of any activity. The use of Computerised Axial Tomography (CAT) scans and Magnetic Resonance Imaging (MRI) has enabled neurologists to demonstrate the effect on the brain of stress. The learner under stress will resort to rote and ritualistic responses, sight or flight responses and be resistant to anything new. In other words, a learner who is under stress will not learn anything as it is biologically impossible!

There are many different ways of relaxing and we each have a way that suits us best. Brain research confirms that as stress increases, the ability to learn decreases, so establishing the right kind of atmosphere is clearly essential to facilitate a successful outcome. Moreover, the current demand for stress management books and courses confirms that knowing how to relax is one of the most useful skills we can learn.

The following exercise is adapted from a suggestion in **The Magical Classroom** by F. Noah Gordon (1995). If practical, ask the students to lie on the floor. They can make pillows to rest their heads on by rolling up a jacket or a pullover. (Words you might like to pre-teach before the exercise: fists / tight / muscles / tense / limp / shrug / stretch / yawn / wrinkle / stiff / sink / curl up.)

> "Move around a bit until you get as comfortable as you can. Now close your eyes and think of your hands ... . Make tight fists with your hands ... as tight as you can. (*Pause several seconds.*) Good, now relax your hands ... and feel the warm tingling sensation you get as your muscles say 'Ahh, we can relax now.' Now bend your arms and make a muscle, making your arms very tense and tight. (*Pause several seconds.*) Now relax and let your arms go limp. Good, now shrug your shoulders ... raising them up to your ears ... and hold them there for a few seconds, tightly. Okay, now let them go and notice how good that feels.
>
> Still keeping your eyes closed, open your mouth wide, until you can feel your face muscles stretch ... like in an enormous yawn ... and close your mouth ... . Now press your tongue up against the roof of your mouth ... and really feel the pressure. Good now let it go and notice how good it feels to relax your tongue again. Okay, now wrinkle up your nose, make a funny face and hold it. (*Pause several seconds.*) Now let it go, and feel your face becoming very smooth and soft.

❖
❖
❖
❖
❖
❖
❖
❖
❖
❖
❖
❖
❖
❖
❖
❖
Now tighten your stomach muscles. (*Pause several seconds.*) Now relax them again ... just let them become soft and easy. Now tense all the muscles of your legs ... as stiffly as you can ... and hold the position. (*Pause several seconds.*) Good. Now relax your legs ... and notice how warm and good they feel, almost like sinking into the floor ... . Now curl up your toes really tight ... hold them in that position ... then relax.

Now ... take three slow, deep breaths, and each time blow the air out so you can hear yourself exhale. Breathe in the warm light, and breathe out all of your tightness ... . Breathe in the warm light and breathe out all of your tightness ... . Breathe in the warm light and breathe out all of your tightness ... . Now open your eyes and smile at someone!"

Two further relaxation techniques are presented below, taken from *Accelerated Learning In The Classroom* by Alistair Smith (1996).

❖
❖
❖
❖
❖
❖
❖
❖
❖
❖
❖
❖
❖
❖
❖
❖
❖
"Firstly close your eyes and then one stage at a time relax each part of your body. Breathe evenly and gently. As you progress, repeat to yourself in a progressively slower monotone: 'Now I relax my eyes ... now I relax my mouth ... now I relax my neck ... now I relax my shoulders ... now I relax my arms ... now I relax my chest ... now I relax my stomach ... now I relax my legs ... now I relax my feet.'"

"Sit or stand in an upright position. Place your clasped hands on your stomach. Breathe evenly and gently. Breathe from your belly first, filling up your stomach and chest like a balloon. Continue to breathe as your chest rises. Continue to breathe into your throat. Then gently exhale. Repeat the exercise. It may help to visualise the air filling up like a balloon as you go."

Autogenic training, the use of mandala, transcendental meditation, or yoga for relaxation can all be made use of for the purpose of creating a relaxing learning atmosphere. In fact, this list of possibilities is endless. The technique below is known as **The Breath on the Left** and it has also been found to be effective:

❖
❖
❖
❖
❖
❖
❖
❖
❖
Sit still in a chair with your spine straight, eyes closed and with your left hand relaxed in your lap. Bring the right hand up and block off the right nostril with your right thumb. Begin long, deep breathing through the left nostril. Relax the abdomen to bring the air into the lower lungs, then expand the chest. Continue the long deep breathing a minimum of twelve times. Then inhale, hold for five seconds, exhale and relax.

If working with adult learners, it is more than likely they will have some techniques of their own and they can lead the class through the exercises instead of you taking centre stage. There can be no greater boost to their confidence than having such opportunities and we should create them whenever we can.

Making use of music can also help to create optimal learning conditions. Teachers frequently give instructions for a particular activity and then tell the class that they have a certain number of minutes in which to complete it. Why? This only puts unnecessary pressure on the group. An alternative is to play background music during the task, then to turn up the volume before fading it to indicate that the time has come to finish. Surely this is preferable to having to bang on the table, clap your hands or shout to gain their attention. Music can also be used to promote the students' self-esteem by playing a fanfare to greet them when they walk into the room for class or recording a burst of applause to play each time they produce a correct response.

Music elicits emotional responses, receptive or aggressive states and stimulates the limbic system. The limbic system and subcortical region are involved in engaging musical and emotional responses. But more importantly, research has documented that the limbic part of the brain is responsible for long-term memory. This means that when information is imbued with music, there's a greater likelihood that the brain will encode it in long-term memory.

Suggestopedia originated with the work of Dr Lozanov, a Bulgarian psychotherapist in the 1970s. It entails the creation of an optimum learning state by removing the barriers to learning and providing a positive expectation of success. The four-phase cycle consists of the Presentation, the Active Concert – the target material read to Classical music, the Passive Concert – the target material read to Baroque music, and the Activation. The purpose of the Presentation is to give a lively overview and to connect the "known" to the "target" material. Although the Suggestopedic Approach has proved to be an effective way of teaching languages, it is controversial and clearly not everyone's cup of tea. However, the first stage of the cycle can be incorporated into more conventional teaching models without causing too much of a shock to the system!

For a Suggestopedic lesson, the classroom would be prepared before the students arrive – the walls would be covered with visuals related to the content of the lesson, music would be playing related to the target material, and the table covered with realia dealing with the content of the lesson. The students walk into the classroom and pick up the objects from the table and start talking about them. The lesson could be about holidays, for example. You could cover the walls with travel posters, play the sound of waves breaking on a beach, and have a suitcase full of holiday items and souvenirs placed on the table. This will create a memorable learning experience that they are unlikely to forget.

Aromatherapy, the use of essential oils, can even have a part to play in setting the scene. Current research says that for mental alertness, it can be helpful to use peppermint, basil, lemon, cinnamon and rosemary. For calming and relaxation, use lavender, chamomile, orange and rose. A few drops of oil can be added to water in a plant spray and this can be used before the students arrive to help create the right kind of atmosphere.

A Provide the learners with an authentic reason for doing the session: in other words, sell the lesson to the class. Whether the material itself is authentic or inauthentic is of little importance. Research indicates that inauthentic material designed by the teacher to cater for the needs and interests of the class is often more popular with students. Moreover, once authentic material is introduced into the classroom setting, it could be argued that it becomes inauthentic in any case.

In recent years a lot of fuss has been made over the importance of using authentic materials in the classroom to help prepare students for the real world outside. But what is authenticity? A piece of creative writing could be authentic in that it represents an honest endeavour on the part of the writer to express his/her intent. But would this meet the requirements of the purist so that it could be regarded as authentic material to use in class if it were written by you or me? The answer is probably no. Moreover, the fact that it could be used to good effect for teaching purposes would appear to be irrelevant. However, what cannot be disputed is the fact that learners could have authentic reasons for wanting to study such material.

Even when authentic materials are used in the classroom, adaptation seems to be inevitable. Teachers constantly change materials to match the needs and interests of their students, just as they often simplify vocabulary, provide numerous definitions, examples, paraphrases, and synonyms, and even do some improvised vocabulary teaching in the process.

It is also worth pointing out that learners tend to find authentic materials less interesting than "artificial" materials and that this could well affect their motivation. As a teacher, you might well be more enthusiastic about something you have created yourself and your enthusiasm is likely to rub off on the students.

It can be argued that what is of real importance is not whether the material itself is authentic but whether the reasons for completing it are. This would suggest that perhaps we have been getting our priorities wrong and that it is time we reconsidered our attitude to and interpretation of authenticity. The alternative is to reject a lot of valuable material that can be put to effective use.

F

The main feature: PPP, ARC, OHE, Test Teach Test or Guided Discovery. Ensure the main feature caters for the three main learning styles (VAK) and/or Gardner's eight intelligence types.

VAK is used in Neuro-Linguistic Programming to refer to the visual, auditory and kinesthetic learning styles. Unless you cater for these styles in the classroom, you can never be sure of reaching all the students in the group. The kinesthetic students, for example, learn through movement. Unless they have an opportunity to do so at some point during the lesson, they are unlikely to get much out of the experience except for a sense of boredom or frustration. A classroom of learners will include twenty-nine percent who are predominantly visual learners, thirty-four percent who are auditory, and thirty-seven percent who are kinesthetic. NLP has successfully demonstrated that communication between two people takes place in the dominant representational system so we need to have a variety of strategies or our communication is largely with only one group.

As well as there being different learning styles, there are also different intelligence types to consider. Howard Gardner, an educational psychologist at Harvard University, has gathered evidence to suggest that there are eight basic types – linguistic, mathematical, spatial, bodily-kinesthetic, musical, interpersonal – the way we relate to others, intrapersonal – our talent to self-evaluate, and naturalist – the way we make sense of the world around us. There follows a list of activities to cater for each of the eight intelligences:

- **Bodily-kinesthetic:** circle dancing / relaxation exercises / brain gym / craftwork

- **Musical:** songs / background music / jazz chants

- **Interpersonal:** groupwork / pairwork / brainstorming /peer teaching

- **Logical-mathematical:** logic puzzles / problem-solving / logical-sequential presentations / guided discovery

- **Linguistic:** group discussions / reading / completing worksheets / wordbuilding games / giving presentations / storytelling / listening to lectures

- **Spatial:** charts / diagrams / mind maps / videos / visualisations

- **Intrapersonal:** project work / self-study / learner diaries / personal goal-setting / reflective learning activities

- **Naturalist:** classifying & categorising activities / background music – in the form of sounds created in the natural world

E

Error correction: self-correction of errors displayed on an OHT by the teacher. As well as being what the learners themselves actually want, this ensures that the focus of the lesson is not on promoting fluency at the expense of accuracy.

We often assume we know what is best for our students without bothering to find out what they would really like. That is why there is a good case to be made for having a "round" at the end of each week to find out how they are feeling and what they would like more or less of. You have every right to participate in this process too and to share your own feelings with the group. After such a feedback session, a programme can be planned for the following week taking everyone's views into account.

The purpose of the "round" or "weekly reflections" is for everyone to ask themselves if they are really getting what they want. And if the answer is "no", the session provides an opportunity to bring about change. A goal is a destination and a plan describes the behaviours used to get there. This feedback session is a time for self-evaluation, to use your intrapersonal skills to look within and to select new behaviours that will enable you and your students to achieve your goals.

A point that is likely to be raised in such a session is that the learners appreciate being corrected in spite of the fact that it is not particularly fashionable these days. Once the Communicative Approach came into being, accuracy was no longer considered to be so important by teachers and the emphasis was placed on getting the students to communicate effectively. This was reinforced with the advent of the Lexical Approach. This implies that we should accept whatever stage of development the students are at and that we cannot expect learners to master third person Present Simple endings before their time, for example. What I would like to suggest is that this is rather a negative attitude to take and that it is based on the ideas of non-practising teachers who are perhaps unaware of how to help students to overcome such hurdles.

Unmonitored communication can take place among learners in the coffee bar outside the classroom without the teacher being present so how can we justify our roles if we do not intervene to deal with errors occasionally? There is no disputing the fact that it can be damaging to interrupt the free flow to point out errors and that this can result in inhibiting the students. However, there is a viable alternative. While monitoring the activity taking place, the teacher can make a note of errors that crop up on an overhead transparency sheet. This can then be flashed up on the board at the end of the session and the learners can be given the opportunity to self-correct and to explain why the change is necessary.

R Review of the teaching points covered in the form of a visualisation or the Passive Concert stage of the Suggestopedic Cycle. Research indicates that eighty percent of new knowledge is lost within twenty-four hours without some form of review. Use the sixty to seventy beats per minute of Baroque music to induce a state of relaxed alertness which engages the conscious and unconscious mind simultaneously.

The following script is an example of what can be used for the review stage of the lesson for work on irregular verbs:

"Make yourself comfortable and close your eyes. Take a few deep breaths to help you relax. You're walking along a beach by the sea in the sunshine. Hear the sound of the waves, feel the sand between your toes and taste the salt on your lips. You stop still for a moment to enjoy the experience. Now you slowly start to walk again and see in front of you an interesting stick lying on the ground. You slowly reach down and pick it up and notice how good it feels in your hand. With this stick you start to write the following words in the wet sand:

read	read	read
put	put	put
write	wrote	written
drink	drank	drunk
see	saw	seen
drive	drove	driven
take	took	taken
come	came	come
eat	ate	eaten
go	went	gone

You stand still for a moment, look at your work and see it's complete. And as you stand there and watch, you feel the sun on your back and you see the waves coming in, slowly washing away your words, so very slowly, bit by bit, first the lower part and then the upper part. And you feel happy inside because you know the words now. It's so beautiful watching the waves, so very relaxing, a moment in time you will never forget.

And now it's time to return, back the same way you came, back to the place where you started. And as you walk back along the sandy beach, you're smiling because you're still enjoying everything you've seen, heard, felt, smelled and tasted. And all these beautiful things you take back with you. Whenever you want or need, you can just return and enjoy this special place again."

The visualisation presented above was adapted from a script in *Target Fluency* by Michael Hager (1994). The list of verbs can obviously be replaced with other items to be learnt, with spelling or with grammar rules, whatever suits your purpose. There is no statistically significant difference between using Baroque and New Age music in the effectiveness of inducing alpha states for learning so there is no harm in experimenting with different forms of background music to accompany the scripts.

Mnemonic devices could also be incorporated into the scripts as an aid to learning in the Review stage of the cycle. OPSHACOM, for example, could be written in the sand to remember the possible order of adjectives before nouns – Opinion, Shape, Age, Colour, Origin and Material.

Appendix: How To Cater For Young Learners

The teaching of English to young learners has become more important in recent years as a result of the introduction of primary ELT in an increasing number of countries.

So how do the needs of young learners differ from those of adults? In the case of five to seven-year-olds, their understanding comes through hands, eyes and ears, so the physical world is dominant at all times. They also have difficulty in differentiating between fact and fiction. However, whether this is a disadvantage or not is open to debate! Most children have the natural ability to store memories by associating them with their senses. Moreover, they also have the natural ability to cross-sense. In other words, they are synesthetes – being able to hear colour, see sound, taste time, and touch aroma. The advantage of being able to cross-sense is that it expands the memory. Unfortunately they tend to lose this ability as it is discouraged or regarded as silly by their parents and teachers. A lot of children tend to have imaginary friends they have dialogues with. Once again, this ability is usually frowned upon so they drop the practice. The result is that by the time we reach adulthood, we need to relearn the skills we were born with. Guided visualisation can be used to cater for this ability inherent in young learners and the script presented on the following pages offers an example. Depending on the level of the class, you may need to do some pre-teaching of vocabulary the students are unfamiliar with.

An Underwater Adventure

Close your eyes and concentrate on your breath. (*Pause.*)
Now imagine that you're walking down to the beach. It's a
beautiful, sunny day, and you can hear the sound of the
waves. (*Pause.*) As you're walking along the beach you notice a trap
door in the sand. You lift the trap door up, and there are stone steps
leading down under the sand. You walk down the steps, feeling
perfectly safe, and find yourself in a long tunnel. You walk through the
tunnel until you come to a room, which looks like a glass bubble.

You realize that you're in a glass room under the sea. Beautiful
coloured fish are swimming outside. You notice that there is a submarine and a diving suit in the room for you to use if you choose. There
is also a comfortable chair with a pillow on it if you feel like sitting
down. You have a minute of clock time, equal to all the time you need,
to enjoy everything you can see, all the wonders of the sea ...

And now it's time to return again. (*Pause.*) You walk back through the
tunnel, up the stairs towards the sunlight. You close the trap door
behind you knowing that you can return here whenever you like. You
leave the beach behind you and become aware of sitting here, fully
present.

I'm going to count to ten. Join me at the count of six, opening your
eyes at ten, feeling fully awake and remembering everything that
happened on your adventure. One ... two ... three ... four ... five ...
six ... seven ... eight ... nine ... ten.

From *Spinning Inward* by Maureen Murdoch (1987)

The younger the learners, the more physical activities they need. The emphasis in most schools is placed on verbal learning and most testing methods are limited to a linear, sequential format geared to verbal content. The result is that visual or kinesthetic students are often labelled "slow learners". However, if children can draw an image, hum it, or move through it first, they may then be able to talk or write about it more easily. Mime stories can be used to help cater for this in which the children act out the story the teacher tells.

Young learners also prefer working alone and can be reluctant to share. Although the use of pair and groupwork increases the amount of Student Talking Time, imposing this arrangement on pupils who are not yet ready for it can only have a negative effect. Groupwork should not be attempted before the children are used to working in pairs and both forms of interaction need to be introduced gradually to ensure a successful outcome.

Eight to ten-year-olds are more able to make decisions about their own learning, and have developed a greater sense of fairness. They are less likely to laugh at others' mistakes, for example. By this stage they know what they do and they don't like about teachers. Nobody likes teachers who lose their work, for example. From these simple likes and dislikes, it's possible to negotiate a contract and to establish a code of classroom conduct which will help to develop rapport. The resulting contract can be displayed on a noticeboard for everyone to see, bearing everyone's signature: "The students of class ... promise ... . The teacher of class ... promises ... ." The activity caters for intrapersonal intelligence as the pupils look within to decide on what they like/dislike and interpersonal intelligence as they discuss which clauses to include in the final document.

They can also generalise and systematise by this age, making use of naturalist intelligence. A **noughts & crosses** card game can be produced to cater for this ability which the pupils can work on in pairs. A set of at least twenty picture cards can be produced which are dealt equally to each player. The children then take it in turns to lay a card in a square on the grid and the aim is to complete a horizontal, vertical or diagonal line to make a family of words. For example, **the sky / eyes / the sea** could form a line as they can all be blue and **a ship / a box / a cup** could form a line as they are all containers.

Instead of relying mainly on the spoken word, most activities for the younger learners should include movement and bring all the senses into play. Variety is also a "must" to cater for their limited concentration spans, not spending too long on any one stage of the lesson.

Outdoor activities provide young learners with an opportunity for movement as well as catering for the naturalist intelligence type. These could include organising a natural scavenger hunt with pupils having to retrieve various objects – a round stone or something shiny, for example. Another possibility is a treasure hunt, with the children hiding the treasure and then writing detailed directions to the hiding place.

A language teaching method that works particularly well with young learners is **Total Physical Response**. The method, which was developed by James Asher in California, parallels adult learning with first language acquisition and emphasises understanding before production. The learners show their understanding of the language input by the physical way in which they respond to it. Examples of this approach put into practice include drawing a picture described in the form of a dictation, acting out a nursery rhyme, making a model out of plasticine as it is being described, and moving objects from one place to another in response to instructions. It clearly appeals to the bodily-kinesthetic intelligence type and provides an effective means of introducing variety into the classroom and so holding the learners' attention. The work of James Asher on TPR reminds us of the power of activity and motion in learning. Most of what we think is important in our lives, what we really know, we have learned through experience, not from a whiteboard or textbook.

An activity greatly appreciated by young learners is storytelling. To ensure that children get maximum benefit out of the process, it is essential to create a friendly and secure atmosphere. If they're relaxed and comfortable, then they are obviously more open to what they are about to hear. The breathing exercise on the following page is taken from *The Magical Classroom* by F. Noah Gordon (1995) and can be used as a relaxation technique when working with children to help establish optimal learning conditions.

"Close your eyes and sit very quietly. Now just listen to your breath. Breathe in ... and ... out. In ... and ... out. Now continue breathing this way, letting go of any thought, feelings and worries you might have. Just listen to your breath as you breathe gently in ... and ... out ... in ... and ... out. Notice the air moving in and out of your nostrils."

Two stories with accompanying lesson plans are presented below which you might like to try out on your classes.

Why The Crab Has No Head

1. Why are we made the way we are? Why does a leopard have spots and why do elephants have trunks? Here's a folk tale from the Philippines which offers an explanation for one of nature's mysteries.

2. *Narrate the story.*

One day God decided to make a crab. He made the body and legs first, and was pleased with the soft colour of its shell. Then he paused, deciding where he would put the crab's head.

But the crab thumped its body impatiently on the sand, already waiting to scuttle away to find a home. "Be patient!" said God. "I have yet to make your head." But the crab only thumped its body harder and waved its legs restlessly in the air. It was telling God to hurry and finish making him.

In exasperation, God put the crab's eyes on one end of its body, saying, "Impatient creature! Here, take your eyes and go!" The impatient crab scuttled away into the sand, without any head. Feeling embarrassed and foolish that he had offended God by his impatience, the crab hid himself in the sand. To this day, he still does so, coming out for air only occasionally.

(taken from *Cordillera Tales* by Maria Luisa B. Aguilar-Carino, 1990)

Working in small groups, invent stories to explain one of the following. If none of the titles appeal to you, then choose one of your own:

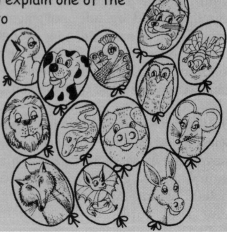

- Why Dalmations Have Spots
- How The Swan Became Black
- Why The Zebra Has Stripes
- How Giraffes Got Long Necks
- Why Polar Bears Are White
- How Camels Got Humps
- Why Hedgehogs Have Spines

The Boy With The Magic Brush

The Boy With The Magic Brush

1. *Show the class the pictures of the paintbrush and palette, the boy carrying a pot of paint in front of his shabby house, a mountain on an island, and a ship on a stormy sea. Then ask them to predict what the story is about while working in small groups. Circulate to provide any assistance required. Invite one person from each group to the front of the room to tell their version of the story to the rest of the class. Make a note of any errors on an overhead transparency sheet. This can be flashed up at the end of the lesson to provide the learners with an opportunity to self-correct. It is not a good idea to interrupt the free flow to deal with the errors during the storytelling.*

2. *Narrate the story* **The Boy With The Magic Brush**.

Once upon a time, in a little village, a poor boy named Ma Liang was born. It was not long before his parents died, so he become an orphan. To survive he had to work for a landlord. He worked day and night.

One day, after finishing his work, he returned to his shabby bed in his shabby little house. When he passed the window of the landlord's house, he saw an artist drawing a picture for the landlord. What a beautiful scene it was! Ma Liang admired it very much. He wanted so much to have a brush to draw with.

"Would you give me a brush to draw?" he asked the landlord.

"You? Ha!" replied the landlord. "A beggar wanting to draw! Are you joking?"

At this, everyone present laughed at Ma Liang. This made him so angry that he made up his mind then and there to learn how to draw. And he vowed to draw only for the poor.

From there on, he began to practise drawing. Whatever he saw and wherever he was, he drew. Because he had no brush, he used a branch or whatever else he could get his hands on. He had no paper, so he often drew in the sand.

Years went by and Ma Liang became a good artist. Everything he drew was as lovely as if it were real. He only wished he had a brush!

One night, after practising drawing, he went to bed. Because he was so tired he began to dream very quickly. Suddenly he was in a different place. A brook led off into the distance with all kinds of flowers on both banks, and an old man stood in front of him. Ma Liang was too surprised to say a word!

" You want your own brush, don't you?" the old man asked.

"Yes, I do!" replied Ma Liang.

"Well then, I will give you a brush, but remember that you promised to draw only for the poor." With this, the old man disappeared.

"But where is the brush?" Ma Liang wondered anxiously. "Where?"

When Ma Liang awoke he realized that it had only been a dream, but to his surprise there was a real brush in his bed. He was very pleased. The first thing he did was to draw a cock on the wall. No sooner had he finished the drawing than the cock stepped out of the wall and came to life. Ma Liang had received a magic brush!

Ma Liang began to draw for the poor. Because he could draw whatever he wanted and whatever he drew came to life, he did a lot of good with his brush. It was not long before the emperor heard the news and ordered his soldiers to bring Ma Liang to him.

The emperor met Ma Liang in his big hall. The emperor said. "I have heard that you have a magic brush that can bring whatever you draw to life. Is this true?"

"Yes," replied Ma Liang.

"Then give it to me," ordered the emperor.

"No, it's mine," responded Ma Liang.

"How dare you say that?" fumed the emperor. "I am the emperor. You must obey me!" At this, two guards snatched the brush from Ma Liang's hands.

The emperor put the brush into the hands of the most respected painter in the kingdom and asked him to draw something, but his painting did not become real. Seeing that his plan was not working, the emperor tried to persuade Ma Liang to draw something. Ma Liang, however, decided to teach the emperor a lesson.

"What would you like me to draw for you?" asked Ma Liang.

"Gold. A hill made of gold," replied the emperor.

Ma Liang began to draw, not a hill of gold, but a picture of the ocean.

"Fool, I want gold!" roared the emperor.

So Ma Liang drew an island of gold in the ocean.

❖
❖
❖ "Now draw a ship," ordered the emperor. A ship soon appeared in the
❖ picture. The emperor hurriedly jumped into the ship with his guards and
❖ prime minister to set sail for the island of gold. The ship sat quietly, so
❖ the emperor once again ordered Ma Liang to draw, this time wind so
❖ that the ship could move.
❖
❖ Ma Liang wasted no time in drawing a
❖ violent wind that almost capsized
❖ the ship. The emperor screamed
❖ for Ma Liang to stop, but Ma
❖ Liang only drew more and more
❖ bad weather until the ship disappeared
❖ out of sight.
❖
❖
❖ Ma Liang continued drawing for the poor. Both he and the poor were
❖ happy.
❖

(taken from *Chinese Folk Tales* by Howard Giskin, 1997)

❖
❖ 3. If I had a magic brush and could make whatever I painted come
❖   true, I'd paint new houses for the homeless and happiness for me
❖   and you.
❖
❖ **What would you paint if you had a magic brush?** *Working in small groups,*
❖ *invite the students to produce a verse like the example to contribute towards a*
❖ *collective poem. This can then be illustrated and mounted on the notice board to*
❖ *decorate the classroom with. The activity provides controlled practice in the use of*
❖ *the second conditional for imaginary situations while the students' conscious*
❖ *attention is deflected from this goal. The result is that the structure is more likely*
❖ *to be retained in the long term memory than it would be if the grammar point was*
❖ *made the main feature of the lesson.*

As an alternative to telling an already written tale, how about creating a story with the
children and then telling it to them? The start of such a process is presented below:

❖
❖ Teacher: When did the story happen?
❖ Pupil: Long before the beginning of time.
❖ Teacher: OK. Long before the beginning of time then. And what
❖   time of the year was it?
❖ Pupil: Summer.
❖ Teacher: So long before the beginning of time in a particularly hot
❖   summer ...
❖

◆ Another storytelling activity is where everyone has two objects or pictures of objects which have to be incorporated into a story. You start the process off and the pupils then take over. As the story continues it gets more and more ridiculous. Writing down the stories they tell helps them to see that print is a means of communication and that there is a relationship between the amount of talking done and the amount of writing on the page. They need to see themselves as writers with something to say.

◆ A topic-based approach to planning a programme of study is recommended as the content of the lessons automatically becomes more important than the language teaching points, which makes it easier to relate the lessons to the experiences and interests of the pupils. Learning takes place indirectly this way and is thus more likely to be retained. Associating words, functions, structures and situations with a particular topic helps memory. It allows you to go into a subject in more depth and brings out reactions and feelings in the pupils which are not always covered in the textbook. This brings the learner and the learners' needs more into focus, ensuring an empowering rather than a teacher-centred approach.

◆ Questionnaires to find out about favourite foods, TV programmes, bedtimes or pocket money can be used. With the five to seven-year-olds you would have to provide the questions but the eight to ten-year-olds would be able to have a go at devising their own with some help from you.

◆ New language can be presented effectively to young learners with the aid of a puppet or cuddly toy. You can use Teddy to ask questions or pupils can ask questions through Teddy. **Teddy wants to know** ... . You can even present dialogues with a puppet or a cuddly toy as your partner.

◆◆◆

Gardner's work on intelligence can profoundly affect the way we view our pupils. People are people and they have the same basic needs and potential talent regardless of their race, ethnic background or economic circumstances. The concept of Multiple Intelligences gives us the possibility of identifying and adapting both the classroom environment and the activities we make use of to cater for these needs and talents. The end result can be that people fall in love with learning instead of regarding the time they spent at school as nothing more than a black cloud that hung over their heads until they came to the end of their prison sentence!

Bibliography

Aguilar-Carino, M. L. B.: *Cordillera Tales* (New Day Publishers, 1990)

Andreas, S. & Andreas, C.: *Change Your Mind And Keep The Change* (Real People Press, 1987)

Beaver, D.: *Lazy Learning* (Element Books, 1994)

Berman, M.: *? R U* (English Experience, 1995)

Berman, S.: *A Multiple Intelligences Road To A Quality Classroom* (IRI Skylight, 1995)

Carter, A. (Ed.): *The Second Virago Book Of Fairy Tales* (Virago Press, 1992)

Castaneda, C.: *The Art Of Dreaming* (Harper Collins, 1994)

Celce-Murcia, Brinton & Goodwin: *Teaching Pronunciation* (CUP, 1996)

Crossley-Holland: *British Folk Tales* (Orchard Books, 1987)

Dennison, P.: *Switching On* (Edu-Kinesthetics Inc., 1981)

Dickinson, L.: *Self-instruction In Language Learning* (CUP, 1987)

Edwards, G.: *Living Magically* (Piatkus, 1991)

Edwards, G.: *Stepping Into The Magic* (Piatkus, 1993)

Eliade, M.: *Shamanism* (Penguin Arkana, 1989)

Fletcher, M.: *The Suggestopedic Elephant* (English Experience, 1995)

Gardner, H.: *Frames Of Mind* (Paladin, 1983)

Gardner, H.: *Multiple Intelligences* (Basic Books, 1993)

Giskin, H.: *Chinese Folk Tales* (NTC Publishing Group, 1997)

Goleman, D.: *Emotional Intelligence* (Bloomsbury, 1996)

Gordon, F. N.: *The Magical Classroom* (Zephyr Press, 1995)

Greenwood, J.: *Activity Box* (CUP, 1997)

Grinder, J. & Bandler, R.: *Frogs Into Princes* (Real People Press, 1979)

Grinder, J. & Bandler, R.: *Trance Formations* (Real People Press, 1981)

Hager, M.: *Target Fluency* (Metamorphous Press, 1994)

Harner, M.: *The Way Of The Shaman* (Harper & Row, 1990)

Henri, A.: *Love Is* (Rogers, Coleridge & White, 1986)

Henri, A., McGough, R. & Patten, B.: *The Penguin Modern Poets: The Mersey Sound*

(Penguin Books, 1967)

Holdway, A.: *Kinesiology* (Element Books Limited, 1995)

Houston, J.: *The Search For The Beloved* (Tarcher, 1987)

Jacobs, J.: *Celtic Fairy Tales* (Dover Publications, 1968)

Jensen, E.: *Brain Based Teaching And Learning* (Turning Point, 1995)

Lacroix, N. & Gallagher-Mundy C.: *Relaxation* (Thorsons, 1995)

Lewis, M.: *The Lexical Approach* (Language Teaching Publications, 1993)

Lewis, M.: *Implementing The Lexical Approach* (LTP, 1997)

Murdock, M.: *Spinning Inward* (Shambhala Publications, 1987)

Palim J. Power P. Vannuffel P: *Tombola* (Nelson, 1992)

Revell, J. & Norman, S.: *In Your Hands* (Saffire Press, 1997)

Scott, W. and Ytreberg, L.: *Teaching English To Children* (Longman, 1990)

Scrivener, J.: *Learning Teaching* (Heinemann, 1994)

Singer & Switzer: *Mind-Play: The Creative Uses Of Fantasy* (Prentice-Hall, 1980)

Smith, A.: *Accelerated Learning In The Classroom* (Network Educational Press, 1996)

White, R. & Arndt, V.: *Process Writing* (Longmans, 1991)

Zdenek, M.: *The Right Brain Experience* (Corgi, 1996)

Crown House Publishing Limited

Crown Buildings,
Bancyfelin,
Carmarthen, SA33 5ND
Wales,
UK.

Telephone: +44 (0) 1267 211880 Facsimile: +44 (0) 1267 211882
e-mail: crownhouse@anglo-american.co.uk Website: www.anglo-american.co.uk

We trust you enjoyed this title from our range of bestselling books for professional and general readership. All our authors are professionals of many years' experience, and all are highly respected in their own field. We choose our books with care for their content and character, and for the value of their contribution of both new and updated material to their particular field. Here is a list of all our other publications.

Change Management Excellence: Putting NLP To Work In The 21st Century
    by Martin Roberts PhD   Hardback   £25.00

Doing It With Pete: The Lighten Up Weight Management Programme
    by Pete Cohen & Judith Verity   Paperback   £9.99

Figuring Out People: Design Engineering With Meta-Programs
    by Bob G. Bodenhamer & L. Michael Hall   Paperback   £12.99

Gold Counselling™: A Practical Psychology With NLP
    by Georges Philips & Lyn Buncher   Paperback   £14.99

Grieve No More, Beloved: The Book Of Delight
    by Ormond McGill   Hardback   £9.99

Hypnotherapy Training In The UK: An Investigation Into The Development Of Clinical Hypnosis Training Post-1971
    by Shaun Brookhouse PhD   Spiralbound £9.99

Influencing With Integrity: Management Skills For Communication & Negotiation
    by Genie Z Laborde   Paperback   £12.50

Multiple Intelligences Poster Set
    by Jenny Maddern   9 posters   £19.99

The New Encyclopedia Of Stage Hypnotism
    by Ormond McGill   Hardback   £29.99

Now It's YOUR Turn For Success: Training And Motivational Techniques For Direct Sales And Multi-Level Marketing
    by Richard Houghton & Janet Kelly   Paperback   £9.99

Peace Of Mind Is A Piece Of Cake
    by Joseph Sinclair & Michael Mallows   Paperback   £8.99

The POWER Process: An NLP Approach To Writing
    by Sid Jacobson & Dixie Elise Hickman   Paperback   £12.99

Precision Therapy: A Professional Manual Of Fast And Effective Hypnoanalysis Techniques
    by Duncan McColl PhD   Paperback   £15.00

Scripts & Strategies In Hypnotherapy
    by Roger P. Allen   Hardback   £19.99

The Secrets Of Magic: Communicational Excellence For The 21st Century
    by L. Michael Hall   Paperback   £14.99

Seeing The Unseen: *A Past Life Revealed Through Hypnotic Regression*
    by Ormond McGill   Paperback   £12.99

Slimming With Pete: *Taking The Weight Off Body AND Mind*
    by Pete Cohen & Judith Verity   Paperback   £9.99

Smoke-Free And No Buts
    by Ann Williamson & Geoff Ibbotson   Paperback   £7.99

Solution States: *A Course In Solving Problems In Business With The*
Power Of NLP
    by Sid Jacobson   Paperback   £12.99

The Sourcebook Of Magic: *A Comprehensive Guide To NLP Techniques*
    by L. Michael Hall   Paperback   £14.99

The Spirit Of NLP: *The Process, Meaning And Criteria For Mastering NLP*
    by L. Michael Hall   Paperback   £12.99

Sporting Excellence: *Optimising Sports Performance Using NLP*
    by Ted Garratt   Paperback   £9.99

Time-Lining: *Patterns For Adventuring In "Time"*
    by Bob G. Bodenhamer & L. Michael Hall   Paperback   £14.99

Vibrations For Health And Happiness: *Everyone's Easy Guide To Stress-free Living*
    by Tom Bolton   Paperback   £9.99

Order form

*******Special offer: 4 for the price of 3!!!*******

Buy 3 books & we'll give you a 4th title - FREE!
(free title will be book of lowest value)

Qty Title

— *Change Management Excellence*
— *Doing It With Pete!*
— *Figuring Out People*
— *Gold Counselling™*
— *Grieve No More, Beloved*
— *Hypnotherapy Training In The UK*
— *Influencing With Integrity*
— *A Multiple Intelligences Road To An ELT Classroom*
— *Multiple Intelligences Poster Set*
— *New Encyclopedia Of Stage Hypnotism*
— *Now It's YOUR Turn For Success!*
— *Peace Of Mind Is A Piece Of Cake*

Qty Title

— *The POWER Process*
— *Precision Therapy*
— *Scripts & Strategies In Hypnotherapy*
— *The Secrets Of Magic*
— *Seeing The Unseen*
— *Slimming With Pete*
— *Smoke-Free And No Buts*
— *Solution States*
— *The Sourcebook Of Magic*
— *The Spirit Of NLP*
— *Sporting Excellence*
— *Time-Lining*
— *Vibrations For Health And Happiness*

Postage & packing

U.K.:	£2.50 per book
	£4.50 for 2 or more books
Europe:	£3.50 per book
Rest of the world	£4.50 per book

My details:

Name: Mr/Mrs/Ms/Other (please specify) ....

Address: ....

....

....

Postcode: .... Daytime tel: ....

I wish to pay by:

❑ Amex   ❑ Visa   ❑ Mastercard   ❑ Switch - Issue no./Start date: ....

Card number: .... Expiry date: ....

Name on card: .... Signature: ....

❑ cheque/postal order payable to **AA Books**

Please send me the following catalogues:

❑ Accelerated Learning (Teaching Resources)
❑ Accelerated Learning (Personal Growth)
❑ NLP
❑ NLP Video Library - hire (UK only)
❑ NLP Video Library - sales
❑ Ericksonian Hypnotherapy
❑ Classical Hypnosis

❑ Gestalt Therapy
❑ Psychotherapy/Counselling
❑ Employee Development
❑ Business
❑ Freud
❑ Jung
❑ Transactional Analysis

Please fax/send to:
The Anglo American Book Company,
FREEPOST SS1340
Crown Buildings, Bancyfelin, Carmarthen SA33 4ZZ, United Kingdom.
Tel: +44 (0) 1267 211880 / 211886 Fax: +44 (0) 1267 211882
or email your order to:
crownhouse@anglo-american.co.uk